THE COFFEE CODE

HOW A SIMPLE MEETING OVER COFFEE CAN INTRODUCE YOU TO A WORLD OF CAREER OPPORTUNITIES

MARC REEDE

THE ESSENTIAL MENTOR PRESS

Copyright © 2024 by Marc Reede

All rights reserved.

No part of this book may be reproduced in any form or by any electronic or mechanical means, including information storage and retrieval systems, without written permission from the author, except for the use of brief quotations in a book review.

The Essential Mentor Press

www.theessentialmentor.com

ISBN 979-8-9910325-0-6

eBook ISBN 979-8-9910325-3-7

Cover by Paul McCarthy

Editor Aaron Reed Wyman

Illustrations Emily Mills

GIVING THANKS

I'd like to acknowledge a special person who doesn't even realize he's my mentor but whose inspiration got me to the finish line.

Kenton Nelson.

Kenton is a famous artist based in Pasadena.

A few years ago, I had the pleasure of meeting him at one of his shows. I told him of my passion for helping young people with their career readiness.

When he heard about my book project, Kenton let me know that when he was 40 years old and working full-time, he dreamed of becoming an artist—a dream that had been with him his whole life.

He shared with me how he achieved it.

He devoted one day a week to his passion, and over time, he was able to start making a living selling his beautiful art.

Kenton advised me that night to find one day each week to make my passion a reality. That's exactly what I've done. This book is the result.

Thank you, my friend.

CONTENTS:

CHAPTER 1
GIVE:
Share your gift with others.................11

CHAPTER 2
BRAND:
Set yourself apart from others..............19

CHAPTER 3
HELP:
Seek advice from those willing to share....61

CHAPTER 4
MEET:
Build your network of contacts............85

CHAPTER 5
WORK:
Consistently perfect your plan............125

CHAPTER 6
FAIL:
Learn from your losses......................201

Let's get into the coffee code!

INTRODUCTION

THE WORLD TODAY

Just when you thought you had that career thing under control, a pandemic struck. Everyone and every business across the globe took a hit. COVID-19 wiped out plans and disrupted livelihoods. For new entrants to the workforce, internships disappeared, job promises were lost, funding vanished, and relationships burned. Uncertainty took the forefront on the global stage.

Whatever you're going through, do yourself a favor and take a breath.

Your aspirations, goals, and dreams haven't left. They just took a break. You have plenty of time to regroup and prepare for the other side of whatever it is you're going through.

And I'm here to help.

For over 30 years, I've been a lecture agent. My job is to place masterful keynote speakers for major companies to inspire their employees to overachieve. These speakers include mentors, authorities, experts, advisors, and influencers. They're the likes of Simon Sinek, Adam Grant, Mel Robbins, the *Shark Tank* Sharks, Malala Yousafzai, Magic Johnson, and even Bill Gates.

I've attended hundreds of these programs alongside these talents. But here's the fun part: I'm backstage as they await the call to take the stage. This invaluable one-on-one time has taken my relationships with these masters of motivation to a much deeper level. I've learned valuable insights, and I'm excited to share them with you.

WHY ME?

I first met Danny Meyer at a keynote speech we booked for him in St. Louis. We became fast friends. Danny's not only the owner of some of the most successful restaurants in New York City but also the founder of the Shake Shack hamburger chain. Danny's book *Setting the Table* is a national bestseller, and he's a noted authority on hospitality and customer service.

When I shared my intent to write this book with Danny, his immediate response was, "Why you?"

That was a good question. So, I began a search within myself to discover my own personal value that I could bring to young talents about to embark on their careers.

As a small business owner, I've always taken an interest in hiring bright minds fresh out of college. When my son and daughter were seniors at USC and Boston College, I was the go-to dad to give life advice to their close friends and teammates. But I realized that my role as an engager of talent better answers Danny's question about my credibility to pen a book on career readiness. Not only do the pages that follow include behind-the-scenes lessons learned from my years as a business owner in a specialized industry, but also, I've asked a number of these influencers for their insights and advice as you embark on one of the most important journeys of your life.

I've unlocked for you a backstage key to enjoy some of America's most influential and brilliant minds.

So that's *why me*, Danny.

GETTING TO HERE

I grew up in Los Angeles and never left. I had many odd jobs during high school and college. I never assumed I'd end up working for a big company, and I was right. My dad had his own company and, I guess, the entrepreneurial route was just in my blood. The one thing I now look back on after this lengthy career is the fact that my ability to quickly make friends and develop lasting relationships was what got me started and keeps me going today.

In fact, it was my first mentor who got me on my path to success. Ed Hookstratten was the father of my best friend Jon when I was an undergrad at UCLA. Ed was an entertainment attorney in Beverly Hills. He represented, among others, Elvis Presley. One of my part-time jobs during college was delivering flowers for a local flower shop, and I was sure excited one morning when my list of deliveries included Ed Hookstratten's home in Bel Air. When he answered the door, Ed immediately recognized me as one of his son's good friends. That afternoon, Jon called me to say that his dad wanted to meet me because he saw something in me that reminded him of himself when he was younger.

Thus began a terrific mentor relationship. Every few months, I'd take the bus from UCLA to Ed's office. I'd sit down and just watch him work with his many clients on the phone. Ed represented nearly every newscaster in LA, and he had three big-screen TVs side-by-side-by-side so he could watch the local news channels simultaneously. If an anchor's tie was tied poorly, Ed went straight to the phone and called the hotline in the studio to make it right. After that next commercial break the tie was straighter than an arrow.

My relationship with Ed took an important turn one afternoon during my senior year. While at UCLA, I'd also befriended some athletes. My good friend Michael Holton was a star on the basketball team. He was about to get drafted into the NBA and he asked me to be his agent. I immediately made a beeline to Ed's office, excited to have him help me enter the world of representing athletes.

Instead (and I remember this like it was yesterday), Ed looked at me and he told me to tell Michael Holton that I was going to law school, and once I graduated, I could represent anyone I wanted.

On solely those words of advice from my mentor, I studied for the LSAT, got accepted to Loyola Law School, and graduated three years later.

So, that's how it all began for me. I promise there's more, and we'll get there soon. But suffice it to say, my mentor's kickstart was all it took for me to eventually start my own business. Now here's where you come in.

This is a young person's world. You see the future differently. You see technology differently. And you've been exposed to influencers who have skewed the norm to a place where the answer isn't "go get a job and work for a big company and have a nice life."

The title "influencer" carries a lot of weight in today's social media-dominated world. But for the sake of this book, let's look at influencers as the authorities, experts, guides, and mentors that they truly are.

An influencer is an entrepreneur, a risk taker, a self-starter. And I'd bet that you see those same traits in yourself when you look in the mirror.

Now, my story ended up taking a bit of a turn from representing athletes, but after starting my own business a few years after graduating from law school, I haven't looked back.

In the pages that follow, you'll not only benefit from my many experiences in business but also from the brilliance and ingenuity of some of the most influential legends of our time—all of whom are tremendously popular motivational speakers and each of whom has something important to share with you as you begin your quest for success. You'll see common bonds between these influencers purely from a "self-motivated" or "self-starter" perspective. These individuals have never waited for the phone to ring; they make it ring. They're self-starters. They wake up early and they're excited for each day's new challenge.

To be successful in today's world, you need to be a good listener and put this advice to good use. While most of these influencers may not have a resume that shows ten or 20 years as an employee who worked their way to the top, at some point, each of these people stood in your same shoes. Don't expect a golden key to unlock the door to immediate success. Each influencer here faced sacrifices and losses and rejections and failures and then successes. It's like that for everyone. Whenever a bump in the road used to disrupt a project or a deal I was working on, I used to say, "That's just life getting in the way." The disruption caused by the pandemic was one heck of a big bump, but believe me, your success will be waiting at the other end of this diversion. It's all about waking up to a sunny day each and every day no matter what it may look like outside.

Hall of Fame Coach Pat Riley was my first client when I started in this industry in the late 1980s. Pat was coaching the "Showtime" Lakers led by Kareem Abdul Jabbar and Magic Johnson. By the time Pat led The Lakers to back-to-back NBA Championships, we'd built his brand on the corporate lecture circuit to a point where he was the most requested speaker in America.

I used to look at the speaking deals we'd book for Coach Riley and other legends of sports and business as simply one-off opportunities for a great speaker to inspire a major company's employees. But what I learned early on were two key business lessons that I adhere to even today:

1. The importance of being a good listener
2. The value of developing relationships in business

I learned this first lesson after Coach Riley had given one of his first speeches for Kawasaki Motors. He told me how much he loved speaking because he got to see in-depth the leadership styles of these company executives in action. He even used some of these learnings with his Lakers players. Something clicked for me in this moment. His willingness to learn inspired me to spend more time at these events myself, just to listen to the wisdom that these influencers shared. It was as if I was the ultimate conference attendee with the ability to get up close and personal with the best in the business at the podium every single day. I took copious notes, and I used what I learned to thrive in a competitive business environment. A Bill Gates keynote speech we booked for Walmart was just one of those memorable bookings.

The second lesson I've now experienced over and over again is the value of just a single relationship in business. The importance of a simple handshake with someone, sending a handwritten note after an in-person or zoom meeting, a text or email just to say hello, these are invaluable touches. These small pings better my relationship with my customers and ensure that I end up with referrals to others who may help me on my journey. Whether it's my vying for the business of a corporate meeting planner, or you getting the attention of a prospective employer or business partner, the game is exactly the same. It's about listening and building relationships.

Finally, before we get going, I want to share one more key lesson Pat Riley taught me about life: *Never pat yourself on the back for a job well done.* In other words: *Accept praise, but don't expect it.* The time you waste waiting for someone to thank or acknowledge you for something you did is a lost opportunity to get the next one. If I do something well, I know I did good and I'm ready to move on to the next one. The next one will always be waiting for you.

Famed Duke Coach Mike "Coach K" Krzyzewski would teach his teams a similar message, albeit for a job not-so-well done. If one of his players made a bad pass or missed a shot during a game, the last thing Coach K wanted to see was that player wasting his time being upset about that last play. To prevent this, Duke bench players chanted "NEXT" whenever there was a miscue.

The chapters that follow highlight a series of inspirational lessons that will lead you through the unsureness of this process and prepare you for your future well beyond. The process is divided into six silos. No one silo is more important than the next, and you'll no doubt see similarities in some of these groupings. In each silo, you'll find my own messages as well as those from key influencers to better your growth during this process.

This is the process:

GIVE: Always share your gift with others.

BRAND: This is the creation of Me, Incorporated. Identify your strengths to better develop your personal brand.

HELP: Find a trusted guide (or guides) to help you through this process.

MEET: Build and maintain a network of relationships. Continually interact with these contacts.

WORK: Undertake this process on *your* terms.

FAIL: Rejection and failure lead to resilience and grit. Watch how a NO can easily lead to a YES.

My goal is simple: to make your transition from college or graduate school to a career less stressful by sharing ideas and lessons learned so you can build a personalized roadmap to success. Enjoy the ride.

A SHORT STORY

Joan Lunden is the former host of ABC's *Good Morning America*. She overcame a highly publicized battle with breast cancer. Joan's a wonderful speaker, and one concept that she tells audiences that sticks with me is that there are two important days in our lives: the day we are born and the day we can go out and impact the lives of others.

I took these comments to heart as I prepared this book. Yes, we are here to find a job, realize our goals, and reach for our dreams, but when you become aware of the power that you have to influence the life of another, this game will take on a wholly different perspective.

Let me share a story.

Tennis got my daughter Casey into the University of Southern California. Her main inspirations were Venus and Serena Williams, both of whom also grew up in LA.

A few years ago, just after she was accepted to USC, Casey and I had the chance to go to the Madrid Open Tennis Tournament.

The Madrid Open is a clay court tournament that leads into the French Open. I'm lucky enough to be friends with tennis star Andy Roddick's agent, and he'd gotten us coach's passes to this prestigious event.

The day before the tournament started, Casey and I decided to go and see just how close our passes would get us. We showed up at the players' registration area. It was a vast indoor two-story lobby. It felt like the lobby of a large convention hotel. The ceilings seemed to go on forever. There were two identical staircases in the middle of the room that led up to the players' lockers, massage area, and restaurant. The room seemed empty. But then, off in the corner of the lobby, I spotted someone I recognized.

It was Richard Williams, Venus and Serena's dad (and their coach at the time).

Since we were both from LA, I figured I'd go over and say hello. After all, here we all were, 6,000 miles from home.

I introduced my daughter and myself to Richard. I shared with him that Casey had just gotten into college to play tennis and that his daughters were the reason she took up the sport in the first place.

His face lit up and he called out for Venus and Serena. Two figures appeared at the top of the stairs, and they immediately came down to greet us. We chatted with them for a bit, and then we went our separate ways.

The next night, Casey and I watched Venus' opening match against a woman from Madrid. I'm pretty sure we were the only Venus fans in the stadium. While we may have been sitting high up in the rafters, whenever Venus made a great shot or an ace serve, there was no doubt where the cheers were coming from. Venus won in straight sets.

If you follow professional tennis, you'll know that when a match ends, the players zip up their bags and go off to their private exit. Casey knew this, and as the crowd filed up the stairs to leave, she ran down the stairs, against the traffic, to get as close as she could to her new friend.

I was still in my seat, focused on Venus as she put her rackets and towels together and zipped up her bag. Venus looked up at me and mouthed: *Where's Casey?*

I was floored.

Not able to see Casey, I pointed to the place I knew she went and watched as Venus got up and ran over. A few minutes went by. It felt like an eternity. But then I caught a glimpse of Casey coming up the stairs. Tears flowed down her eyes. In her hands was Venus' tournament towel.

As we left the stadium, we ran into Richard Williams in the lobby. I shared this story with him, and he took Casey and me into a group hug. He told us that by sharing a moment with Casey, Venus had done her job. He continued to explain something that has shaped my life even to this day. He shared that he taught his girls to touch just one person in life, to show them that you care, to share your gift, and that you'll be amazed by what can happen.

I tell this story because your job is to look at your many gifts and find a way to share them with others who may turn to you for inspiration. The payback to you will be priceless.

Now, let's get to work.

TIME TO FOCUS

You're about to dive into a process that's not even close to a one-time occurrence. You'll learn how to build and develop your team of mentors, and you'll prepare yourself to be as attractive as possible to a unique set of suitors. As a result, you'll get interviews and job offers.

You'll walk away from this book with a better feel of your purpose. There will be some "big picture" revelations that will take time to sink in—especially as you begin to develop your brand. Remember, these lessons need to be read, re-read, and mastered. It will take time. Take the advice in this book seriously. It's meant to help you succeed.

REMEMBER

Life isn't just about what you get, it's also about what you give. Don't forget to share that gift with others.

CHAPTER TWO:

BRAND

SET YOURSELF **APART** FROM THE REST

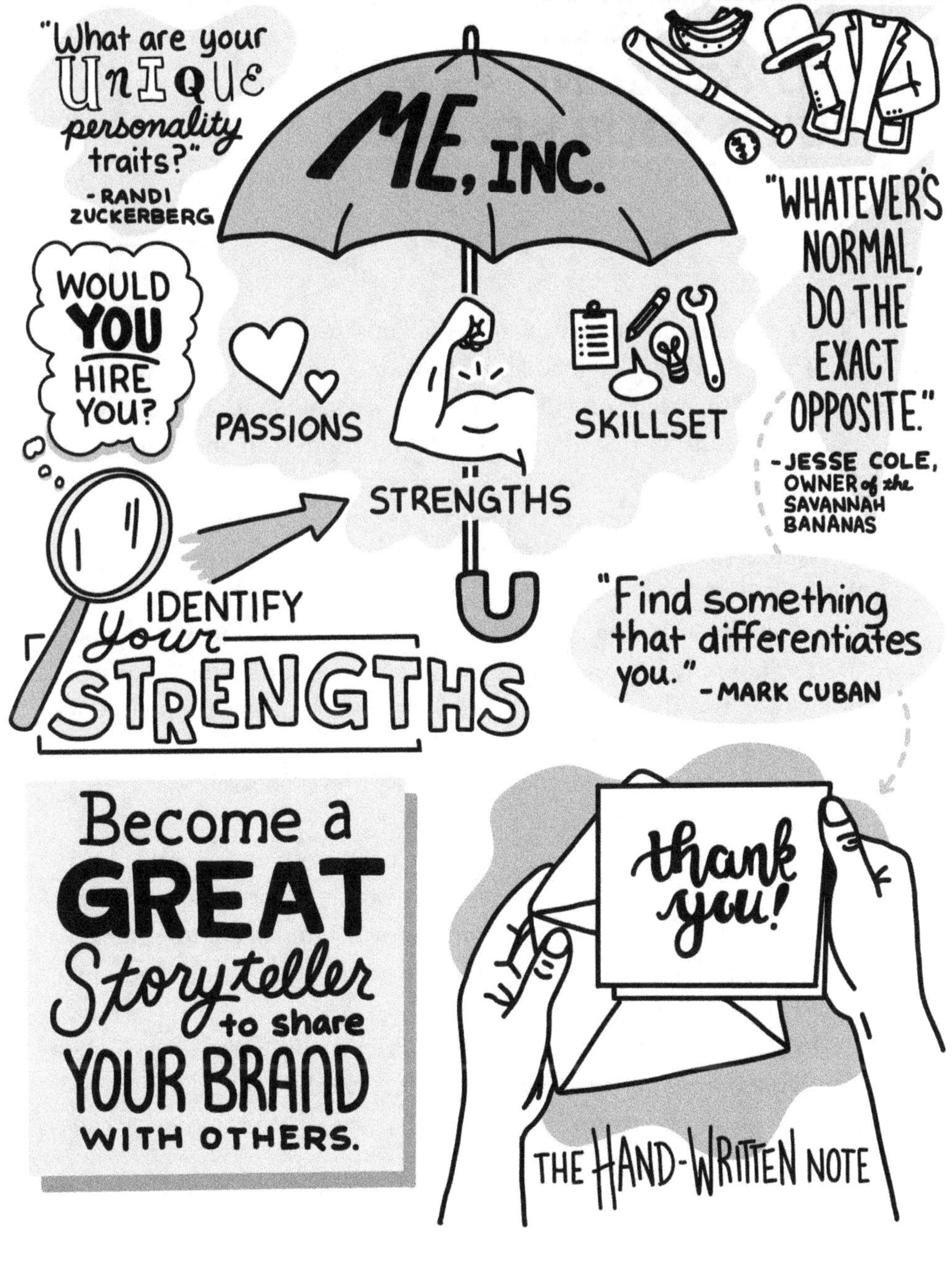

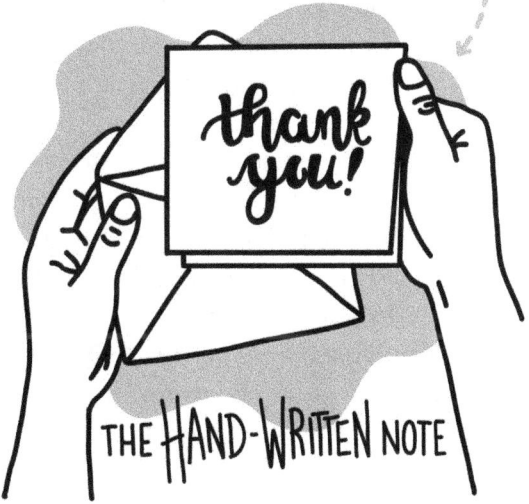

THE VALUE OF STORYTELLING AS YOU BUILD YOUR BRAND

Let's think about that Venus Williams story for a minute. For me, that simple story about a young (albeit famous) woman and her father has provided me with strength and compassion. Witnessing this story's impact on others inspired in me a lifelong desire to help others.

Why does this matter?

Well, a story well told may just be the distinguisher for you to get this job.

When interviewing, you find yourself in a position where you need to not only impress a prospective employer or business partner or investor, but also you need *the memory of you* to stick with them well beyond your first meeting.

To do this, you need to develop a story about yourself.

What is the adventure that *is* your life?

It doesn't have to be long. It simply needs to be memorable and leave the listener with a sense of who you are. Once you've developed that story and have written it down, you need to practice telling it over and over and over again until it just flows, and you leave your audience wanting more.

I want you to think about what *your* Venus and Casey story looks like. Discover a story that reveals you that can be told in an easy to listen to way. Try to find one with characters your audience can

THE COFFEE CODE

relate to and root for. Crafting and practicing this *can* make the difference in your next meeting. It can get them invested in what you're sharing, whether it's the deck for your startup, the reasons you're the right hire for them, or the importance of having you as a partner on a project.

As you prepare yourself to master these interviews and coffee meetings, you'll need to arm yourself with what I like to call *Me, Incorporated*.

As you discover and craft this narrative, remember that there is nobody quite like you.

Mark Cuban, the media entrepreneur who's best known for his role on *Shark Tank* and as the owner of the Dallas Mavericks, has two powerful thoughts on selling yourself that are worth remembering.

1. **Don't sell your product, solve their problem.** Mark Cuban frequently speaks about the importance of putting yourself in the shoes of the person to whom you're selling. And you're always selling, whether it's to prospects, investors, or employees.

2. **Point out what makes you unique early on in communication.** Mark gets up to 1,000 emails each day. Most people are pitching him ideas that he does read, but 90% are *"delete, delete, delete, glance, and delete."* Getting Mark Cuban's attention is simple: Get to the point. He finds that, frequently, the longer the back story someone provides, the worse the deal will be.

Let's look a bit deeper at number one above. If you're searching out employment and going through the interview process, remember that it is NOT about you. This process is ONLY about the company you're looking to join and how you can help them. As you sell yourself to these people, show them why having you on their team makes sense to them now and in the future.

Building Me, Incorporated is all about making, developing, and fine-tuning your own personal brand. It's a brand that's special to you because you're one of a kind. You have special attributes, training, skills, interests, pursuits, and strengths that your classmates (or others vying for this specific opportunity) don't have. And in your interview, you need to make these qualities known.

Randi Zuckerberg is another accomplished business motivational speaker. In 2004, Randi was enjoying a great job in marketing at an advertising agency in New York City when her brother, Mark, called her from Northern California asking for marketing help with his new company. Randi thought she'd spend just a week helping Mark and his three programmer friends. A week turned into ten years.

Randi Zuckerberg's successes at Facebook, and in her personal business endeavors in the years since, have given her the ability to understand what it takes to succeed in a crowded and competitive world.

I asked Randi for her advice about creating Me, Incorporated. Here's what she shared: "Everyone should be thinking about creating their own personal brand. Of course, you can work for a company or a startup, but the one thing that you carry with you through your whole career is your brand. That's what's going to make other people want to work with you, for you…it's going to bring you clients, money and attention. So, start thinking about how you can create a smart strategic brand. What is that thing that you are uniquely an expert in or unique personality traits that you have that you can really market into something for your entire career?"

CREATING YOUR BRAND

Even though you may not yet know what interests you out there, you're developing a plan that will lead to success. Creating your own brand will give you the chance to stand apart from the rest. This is where you'll discover your strengths, accept the fact that competition is right around the corner, and be called upon to be a leader. Creating your brand is the next step in this process, and you should feel free to lean on your mentors and your friends for their input on how best to leave your mark.

ME, INC.

The only way to stand out in this world is to brand yourself.
Whether you're interviewing for a job or trying to make a big sale, you need to build Me, Incorporated.

As a junior tennis player looking for a place on a Division 1 College tennis team, my daughter found herself in elite company. However, she needed to gain an edge with college coaches that she couldn't quite find on the court.

So, she developed a plan to brand herself. She consistently emailed coaches about her match results and upcoming tournaments and events she'd be attending. She had her name emblazoned on her tennis bag so nobody could miss her as she showed up at high-level tournaments.

As a result, coaches responded positively, and the idea paid off with multiple offers to join some exclusive NCAA Division 1 tennis programs.

ACTION ITEM
Figure out a way to separate yourself from others applying for this same opportunity.

CREATE RAVING FANS

Jesse Cole is a true entrepreneurial visionary. He purchased a fledgling minor league baseball team (The Savannah Bananas), and then, to further affirm his commitment to Savannah Georgia, he bought the stadium they play in.

Jesse's goal: Create Raving Fans.

With guts, creativity, a bit of wackiness, a "never say die" attitude, and a fully mortgaged life, Jesse quickly turned The Savannah Bananas into one of the most entertaining sports teams and experiences in America today.

Their exhibition games are played against the same team over and over in sold-out stadiums across the country, and as Jesse says in his talks, "we're in a league of our own."

Jesse's players dance on the field before the pitcher makes a pitch. Batters come to the plate in stilts. A foul ball caught by a fan means that the hitter is out. It's just a bunch of goofiness that's so over-the-top that The Savannah Bananas have now welcomed more than a million fans to their home ballpark. There's even a 90,000-person waiting list to get season tickets, and they have more TikTok views and Instagram followers than many professional sports teams.

Jesse's mantra is: *Whatever's normal, do the exact opposite.* He believes that to be successful, you need to stand out and be different. Yes, this

THE COFFEE CODE

is an extreme example, but you need to create buzz about yourself. All it takes is some creative thinking and a belief in yourself.

WRITE A GREAT LETTER: HOW I ALMOST WENT TO USC LAW SCHOOL

The ability to write a terrific letter (one that will be *remembered*) is a lost art. People are in such a rush today that short emails, texts, and abbreviated notes are acceptable in business. But they shouldn't be.

A creative and properly crafted letter will be seen, remembered, and, if followed up properly, will be acted on.

My law school admissions experience was directly related to a single letter. I'd just graduated UCLA with a 3.5 GPA, I scored in the 85th percentile on the LSAT, and I'd been accepted to Loyola Law School. But the thing was, I really wanted to go to USC.

So, I wrote the admissions letter of my life.

When USC called me in for an interview, I knew my grades, and even my LSAT scores, were too low to get in. But as I sat down in front of five admissions officers, the lead interviewer told me that they had just wanted to meet the person who wrote the letter.

Now, I didn't get into USC's Law School, but I sure learned a lot that day about just how far our own words can take us.

ACTION ITEM
Identify someone today to whom you can send an awesome letter. Send it.
Then make this a regular process.

THE HANDWRITTEN NOTE

It doesn't matter that when I started my business over 30 years ago, we had no computers, faxes, texts, or email. Every new lead I met, every business customer I sold, every person I felt was good for my ever-expanding circle of contacts deserved a handwritten thank-you note for their courtesy and interest. One of my favorite tools of my trade was my first Mont Blanc pen.

I've been the recipient of some of these notes myself. And, in fact, some of them I've framed in my office. But the one thing I can assure you about that handwritten note is that it's a rarity today. Use that rarity to your advantage and stand out amongst the competition because of it.

ACTION ITEM
Go to your local stationery store and pick up a dozen classy 5x7 note cards with envelopes. If you have the funds available to order personalized note cards with your name embossed across the top, do it.

WHAT IS SUCCESS AND HOW DO YOU KNOW WHEN YOU'RE SUCCESSFUL?

My definition of success: **Self-determined goals achieved in a multitude of ways over time.**

Your definition of success will be different from mine. And no doubt, it will change many times over your life. Success is not the same for everyone. We all dream differently. However, I have one suggestion for your definition of success if it's not already there.

Fit *happiness* into your definition of success.

Some people never stop their pursuit of success, even though they may be mega successful. Think Oprah, The Rock, Mark Cuban—even The Kardashians. Once these people reach a goal, it's like a paper-thin ceiling. They break through and are on to the next goal.

There's nothing to stop you from sharing that same attitude and those same dreams.

ACTION ITEM
What's your definition of success?

TAKE THAT FIRST STEP

The path to your dream job or favorite career can start with something that has seemingly nothing to do with what you aspire to achieve.

It's all about taking that first step.

You may not know what you want to do when you grow up, but every single step along the way will be a learning experience for you.

Here's the kicker: This step might be forwards. It may be backwards. It could even be sideways. It could be the decision to go to grad school, take the realtor exam, or even start your own business.

Now, this step may land you waiting tables at a restaurant. But whatever that first step becomes, take it, and be proud of it.

Anything you choose will give you the ability to meet people and get a better understanding of the world around you. It will help give you certainty in uncertain times. It's a choice that will take you to a new level with new people and new goals. And someday, you'll look back at that step and realize you couldn't have gotten *here* without having done *that*.

TREAT PEOPLE THE WAY YOU WANT TO BE TREATED

As a 27-year-old restaurant owner beginning his career, Danny Meyer got a rude awakening after he had just opened his first restaurant in New York City.

The famed French chef Julia Child came into Danny's Union Square Café with her party one night. Danny was blown away by the appearance, especially since his wasn't a French restaurant (a typical choice for Julia Child). Danny spent most of the night indulging that table's every need and desire.

The next day, Danny received a hand-delivered letter from the Desk of the Editor at *The New York Times*. How exciting for a young restauranteur to be visited by one of the most famous chefs in the world—and now be recognized with a letter from one of the most important publications in America.

Danny opened the letter and all he needed to read was the first line: "Dear Danny, Last night in your restaurant, I too was one of your guests…"

Everyone deserves to be treated special. Go out of your way to show others you care.

DON'T LISTEN TO THE NOISE

Let's face it, you're entering a competitive environment where a lot of talented young people are striving for work in the same field or at the same company.

You want to be a sportscaster?

Studies show that Sports Broadcasting is one of the top fields of interest for college grads. And it's not just a targeted field for young college grads...

How do you handle this?

Put your blinders on. Don't listen to nor pay attention to the noise of naysayers or the competition. Work as hard as you can to land that opportunity. But don't ignore the reality of the situation.

Knowing that others are in pursuit of the same role will make you a better candidate. You might remake your promo tape. You might change the way you market yourself. You might decide to broaden the net of sports teams and networks and TV and radio stations and production companies that you approach. You might realize that having a job as a sales intern at a major league baseball team could potentially land you a role on their local TV or radio production team that could turn this dream into a reality for you.

You've learned the tricks to get there. It will happen for you. You've just got to enjoy this ride.

In my business, I've never listened to the noise of competition. I know who my competitors are and what they do to be successful, but that's the extent of it. If I worried about my competition each day, I'd make no deals. I'd waste my time focusing on the wrong things.

Listening to the noise changes your focus. Your attention is best directed toward making yourself more competitive.

CASEY NEISTAT'S BRAND

Casey Neistat became one of the first social media creators by defining his brand on his terms. He dropped out of high school, moved to New York to become a filmmaker, and now produces entertaining and motivational videos that are viewed by millions.

Casey didn't follow the "normal" route to filmmaker by going to college and then film school. Branding himself as a "storyteller," he created his opportunity in a different way.

Your path to your brand has the added value of your educational achievements. Anything creative that you can add to that brand is a *bonus* to a prospective employer or business partner.

IDENTIFY YOUR STRENGTHS AND SHARE THEM

As I meet college juniors and seniors on the campuses I visit as a speaker, I consistently find that I meet students with the same goals and objectives but with vastly different skillsets.

From a work skillset standpoint, I've watched my son Ryan grow from a Computer Science major at Boston College into a Virtual Reality, AI, and Computer Programming expert. But these are skills that he's expected to have a vast knowledge of when applying for a specific role at a company.

You, no doubt, have the same type skills in your current field of interest. The skills—or strengths—that I'm referring to here are more about your hobbies or your enjoyments away from the business world.

You've acquired special skills in your life that will no doubt help you to stand out amongst the competition in your continuing job search (music, dance, performance, sports, and so much more). If there's a chance that mentioning these strengths in an interview will help, by all means, talk about them. Make sure to add this set of skills to your resume and do some research on the company you're meeting with to see if their executives share some of the same outside strengths that you have.

Let's say you were a college runner or an active marathoner. How many executives in business are marathon runners, bike enthusiasts, swimmers, or ironman competitors? In this health-conscious world, a lot of them! That connection may take you far. And remember, many companies have sports teams that play in leagues against other companies, and your background may just give them, and you, a competitive edge.

ACTION ITEM
Identify two interests you have that potential employers should know about. Write out a sentence or two describing why it might be relevant to them.

WHAT A PERFECT TIME IT IS RIGHT NOW

As you begin this exciting career journey, you won't realize it, but you have a lot more time on your hands now than you'll ever have. Let's maximize this available time today.

EVERYONE'S DIFFERENT

Those people interviewing for this same job each have their own strengths, weaknesses, emotions, and challenges. They've all dealt with their share of life's lessons that have made them stronger—or perhaps even weaker.

Your life lessons to date have molded you into your own person. And something about the person whom you have become will be attractive to an interviewer.

ACTION ITEM
**Make a list of the key differences
that set you apart from others.**

BEYOND JUST YOUR BACKGROUND, STRIVE TO SET YOURSELF APART FROM THE REST

I'm the owner of a small business, so I'm constantly looking to add to my brand. By doing something different from my competitors, I know that I have a chance of standing out.

I try to treat each customer as if they are my *only* account, and I make sure they understand that getting their business matters more to me than anything.

Look at what others are doing to get seen by potential employers. Figure out how you can be a bit different. It gets noticed.

MAKE A LIST AND CHECK IT EACH DAY

I keep a pad of paper next to my bed at night and on my desk in my office. Some things just need to be on that list, so I don't forget them, and some are action items that I plan to attack the next day.

Your list of things you need to do may sometimes be short. Sometimes it will be two pages. But the point is, by always having a list of action items close by, you'll be setting yourself up for future success. You'll never find yourself asking: *What's next?*

That list may just be your key to not only staying organized, but also to your future successes.

ACTION ITEM
**Come up with five items that must
be on your to-do list right now.**

TRY TO MAKE A GOOD IMPRESSION

Whenever you pick up the phone, shake a hand, send an email, or publish a post, try your best to make a good impression.

If you've ever said to yourself, "Should I really do that?" when it comes to going the extra mile to get noticed by a recruiter or interviewer or another, the answer is YES.

But if you decided not to do it this time around, or you just forgot to do it, just move on. Nobody notices when you omit that special touch, but everyone notices an addition.

STAND OUT FROM THE CROWD: SAM'S PROCESS

One of the students I mentor, Sam, is a recent graduate of The University of Louisiana at Lafayette. When he applied for a manager's position at a company in Dallas, he knew he'd have to stand out as he'd only held associate roles out of college. In addition to his cover letter and resume, Sam created a "My Work in Numbers" graphic that highlighted his significant achievements and work experience. Using this creative approach, Sam knew he could prove his value to this company in a quantifiable way. The one-page piece led to more in-depth interviews for Sam, and he landed the job.

STAND OUT FROM THE CROWD: MIA'S PROCESS

Another student I mentor, Mia, is a senior at Loyola Marymount University. She's a Film major with an emphasis on Broadcast Communications and Marketing.

Mia took the concept of personal branding to the next level by building her own creative website highlighting a portfolio of her work, as well as hosting her own podcast. Mia's website got the attention of executives at Wieden+Kennedy Advertising in her hometown of Portland, Oregon and she received not only a series of direct messages on LinkedIn from these execs, but it also led to a summer internship that may well lead to a full-time offer.

MUST I OUTWORK THE COMPETITION?

Let's say that you took either Mia or Sam's approach to creative branding. The fact that you may have only sent out 20 resumes and cover letters while another student sent out 50 conventional letters is of no consequence. Your 20 tailored and custom-branded proposals took a lot more time to prepare than those 50. Chances are you'll likely see positive results much sooner than the other applicant.

Sometimes working *harder* means working *smarter*.

TARGET A "REACH" JOB

When you applied to college, you no doubt applied to multiple schools—some more likely to accept you than others. It's the same with getting a job. Target Sony Studios, but apply to Disney, Paramount, and Universal Studios as well. Target a specific Ad Agency or Talent Agency but hit everyone.

The loftier the "reach" is, the harder you need to be prepared to work to get the first interview and then get that acceptance. THIS is when you call in those favors from your parents, your friends, your professors—and that network from LinkedIn and more connections you've developed recently.

ACTION ITEM
Make a list of your reach jobs.

ENJOY THE FRUITS OF A VICTORY, JUST NOT FOR TOO LONG

Hall of Fame Basketball Coach Pat Riley was my first client. I still have a framed note from Pat when he recognized a major win we had together over 30 years ago. What stuck out to me to this day from that congrats note is how Pat ended this piece. Pat wrote: *Now get back to work!*

It's so important to understand that you're often only one step ahead of the competition. Every company you meet with understands this, and you need to as well. The world you're about to enter is the ultimate competition, and you need to be prepared. Stay locked-in to a "moving forward" path.

DON'T THE RESUMES OF ALL 22 YEAR OLDS LOOK THE SAME?

Employers know that the references on your resume are effectively a list of part-time employers you've had along with a list of your family's friends. But now here you are—sitting across from an interviewer who's looking at that list.

You need to take that preconceived notion and change it positively for yourself. It's up to you to strive to be different and set yourself apart from the rest. Let that interviewer know how your experiences have prepared you for this position. And, yes, many of these resume references may have been from people you know. But *you* were the team player who showed up early and left late and made an everlasting impression on all involved. Remember to imagine the tables are turned during an interview, and consider the question: Would you hire you?

WOULD YOU HIRE YOU?

Companies that arrange interviews are not just going through the motions for fun; the interview process is taken very seriously at the corporate level. It's an expensive undertaking and these companies are searching for those they believe to be top talent to fit into their company culture, and much more.

It's important for you to take an honest look in the mirror and put yourself in the seat of that person interviewing you. Ask yourself some key questions:

- Have I studied this company? Do I understand what they do, and am I prepared to handle a role here?

- Am I someone this organization needs, or do I just need them?

- Why would I be an awesome hire and a tremendous asset to this company?

- Can I visualize myself coming to work here each day and adding value?

- Am I prepared to be Employee of the Month?

- What's on my resume that needs to be highlighted for this job?

- If the tables were turned and I were listening to myself, would I make the decision to go with me?

ACTION ITEM
Before you walk into any interview, memorize a list of reasons why you would be an asset to this firm. Change your resume to be more job-specific for this company.

SETTING YOUR AIM

When you were younger, you likely participated in five different sports. Then because of several factors that included the time involved, your talents, your passions, and certainly the competition, you cut this list down to one or two.

This same thinking holds true in the job search process. Look for an opportunity that plays to your strengths but keep to an underlying goal of learning more and getting better at any opportunity you choose.

YOUR NEW BUZZWORDS

Persistence. Passion. Focus. Belief. Preparation. Kindness. Understanding. Opportunity. Luck. Choice. Diligence. Relationships.

THE CEILING ABOVE YOU IS MEANT TO BE BROKEN

They say that records in sports won't live on forever. You've no doubt witnessed records dropping like flies over the years.

Don't ever let anyone tell you the limits of what you can do.

That ceiling above you is just temporary.

A passion for winning and a belief in yourself will take you to limits you never imagined existed.

TRUE TALENT TAKES TIME TO SHINE

If you played sports when you were younger, you noticed that some kids were instant stars while others took years to get there. But there was a place for everyone.

The same rules apply here.

You'll meet those who seem to land every interview and get multiple job offers. But then *your* opportunities will start to flow in, and you'll soon realize there's a place for everyone. Over time, your skillset will continue to sharpen.

Patience is the key.

SHARE YOUR PASSION

Your confidence in your abilities is incredibly important at this stage of your life.

Confidence fuels your passion.

If you are passionate about something, people can see this through your body language, your facial expressions, and your overall demeanor. An interviewer who can tell that you're fully invested will believe in you.

Sharing your passion is the best way to add raving fans to your new network of contacts.

THERE'S NO TIME TO BE DISCOURAGED

Most interviewers see so many applicants that they only have time to call back their top candidates.

Most of the coffee meetings you'll get will be with people who took valuable time from their busy schedules to shake hands with you and offer advice.

There's an art to getting meetings, and you may have just unlocked the door to an attribute you'll value for years to come.

YOUR ATTITUDE NEEDS TO REFLECT YOUR VALUE AS AN ASSET

Tommy Lasorda was the long-time Dodgers Manager and a great motivational speaker. He'd often tell the story of the players on his field and how every time a batter came to the plate, each Dodger fielder would say, "I want you to hit the ball to *me*."

There's no reason to ever dodge any opportunity. Be the one who everyone turns to when they need to get the job done. *That's the attitude you need in the business world.*

WORK AT YOUR OWN PACE

You're about to step into a fast-paced society, made even faster depending on the job you choose or the city in which you choose to live. Be comfortable working at your own pace and not someone else's.

REMEMBER

In this chapter, we learned the importance of creating your own personal brand by identifying your individual strengths and then building a story that defines this uniqueness about you.

We now better understand the preparation needed to impress an interviewer and the key of focusing on *your* passions, *your* strengths, and *your* skillsets above anyone else's.

HELP IS ON THE WAY: SOME PERSPECTIVES ON MENTORS

Guidance. Coaching. Assistance. Advice. Mentorship. Outsiders can be invaluable on our path to success.

Key influencers, like Magic Johnson, swear by their first mentors who gave them direction in life. While I'll always credit my business successes to time spent with my first mentor in college, the notion of mentors and guidance for young people in need has certainly changed in recent years.

Social media, online content, podcasts, interviews, and so much more has put these potential mentors in a quasi-personal relationship for so many.

Here's what I mean: Hugely popular influencer and motivational speaker Gary Vaynerchuk (Gary Vee) is followed by millions in search of that extra push. Gary is asked multiple times each day to be a mentor. His response to these people is unequivocally *no*. Gary feels that asking for something so amazing from someone that is their time and energy is *insanity*. He shares that most people who become mentor-hungry are actually using this as an excuse *not* to do their own work. Obviously, Gary Vee questions the need for guidance when he feels maybe you can take that next step on your own. But as you read on, you'll soon understand that Gary's take may have traction.

Similarly, entrepreneur/best-selling author/marketing genius Seth Godin is asked every day to act as someone's mentor. Even if he wanted to, there just aren't enough hours in the day for Seth to accept all of those requests. But maybe it's not about those hours.

Godin explains, "To the hustle people: go find yourself a mentor. That mentor will look out for you. That mentor will pull you along. That mentor can change everything. If you can find someone like that, please by all means…But let's do the math. For every successful person in the public eye, there's 2,000 people who want that person to be their mentor. Mentors don't scale. The alternative is to find heroes and they don't even need to know you exist. You can ask yourself 'What would Susan do? What would Tracy do? What would Bob do?' And use their voice in your head as a compass to help you go on a path. Because heroes are easy to find and they scale like crazy and that's before you hide by saying 'well the reason I'm stuck is because I don't have a mentor,' maybe what you ought to do is identify whatever heroes you want to assemble as your advisors, you find those heroes and then start."

You might be starting to notice a pattern here.

Then there's Chris Do. As a filmmaker and designer, Chris Do's accolades are too numerous to mention and now he's on a path to change the world. Chris founded The Futur, an online education platform with the goal of teaching one billion people how to make a living doing what they love. Chris also chimes in on this issue of non-personal side mentorship and how this can be seen as a good thing. "There's a lot of mentors out there potentially, but not all of them are going to say yes to you," he explains. "Not all of us have access to mentors and it's not realistic that you can call up Mark Cuban or anybody and say, 'will you mentor me?' Because they get asked this all the time by a lot of different people. So, what you want to do is you want to read biographies and stories about successful people—people that you look up to, people who have accomplished things in life who are very optimistic, watch their videos, read their stories, watch their interviews, do all of those things so that your mind will change."

Sounds a lot like Seth Godin's "heroes" idea.

Should this change the way you look at finding that perfect mentor?

While the personalization may be lacking a bit here, this is just another reason for you to continually be creative and be thinking outside of the box.

ALEXIS OHANIAN ON MENTORSHIP

Alexis Ohanian is the founder of Reddit. I'd initially asked Alexis to share his mentor story here but he refused—saying that he never had a mentor when he began *his* career.

But Alexis recently started a new platform he calls The Grand so young people can be at their best in their professional development. The Grand takes the idea of mentorship to an elevated level. It's a group setting in which you're working with a group of six to eight of your like-minded peers who can give you diverse perspectives and opinions. This is in addition to the ongoing coaching that you'll receive through The Grand.

As Alexis now shares, "Coaching has always been something that I have always been very supportive of. I didn't actually get my first executive coach until I came back to Reddit as Executive Chairman back in 2004. I wish I had gotten one sooner. I think I would have made so many better decisions in my career for the first decade had I seen and worked with a coach sooner...I believe we're going to have more effective and happier workforces if people are doing this kind of professional development regularly, as early as possible in their careers. I wish I had done it sooner."

THERE'S NO REASON TO GO IT ALONE

Your career is *not* a process that you'll want to embark on alone, and help is a lot closer than you think. But understand that you'll find varying levels of assistance out there; some will be overly eager to lend a hand, while others will have minimal time to share. So, ask wisely.

Your mentor will provide guidance to you, but that mentor is unlikely to be the person you're currently asking for a job (although you never know until you ask).

Look at a mentor as a counselor for your future. I met with my first mentor regularly because he enjoyed my willingness to listen and learn, and I felt that I always had someone in my corner who I could turn to.

NO MENTOR YET? DON'T STOP YOUR PROCESS

Finding a personal mentor can be a long, arduous task. Don't let the frustration of not having a trusted guide in place slow you down.

This will be a process.

Once you can realize the value of selecting influencers, mentors, or heroes who may not know you personally, but who may have embarked on similar paths to yours, this job gets a lot easier. By taking the time to research and learn what makes these people tick —through interviews, podcasts, books, TED Talks, X (formerly known as Twitter) feeds, Instagram, and so much more accessible to you right now—you'll be prepared with more advice and guidance than you ever realized.

As The Futur's Chris Do says, "Don't get me wrong—if you can find a mentor and one agrees to coach you and help you, fantastic! But don't let that be the thing that gets in the way of doing what you need to do. Because you don't need a mentor when you can have many heroes."

THE ONLY PERSON WHO CARES ABOUT YOU IS YOU

This is a time when all college seniors are asking for favors and looking for help. And I'm sure you realize that it's just a bunch of overlapping requests. You really want to get this job done? Don't rely on anyone but yourself.

EVERYONE NEEDS THE ADVICE OF A MENTOR

I watched a recent Conor McGregor UFC fight from Las Vegas. I'm no big UFC fan, but I enjoyed the excitement surrounding any match with Conor. This one lasted only 40 seconds, but the true surprise was what happened *after* the fight.

Conor's team streamed into the ring to congratulate him. The first to hug Conor wasn't his wife. It was Tony Robbins. Yes, *that* Tony Robbins, the seven-foot-tall motivational icon and life coach, who has self-proclaimed that he's inspired over 50 million people to succeed over his career.

What strikes me about this relationship is that Conor is known to be the best there is. Why should the best need advice and guidance and support?

Turns out that Conor McGregor forged a bond with this ultra-life coach to help him gain a mental edge over his opponents. Because everyone in that ring has similar skills, the realization was that winning is a state of mind.

This is why we all need mentors and people to help guide us in our lives—especially as you step from school into your career.

You'll no doubt be coming up against those with similar skills and backgrounds in job interviews and potential business dealings, but the necessity to shine and find your strengths within may require someone standing outside the box. Because someone looking at you and your situation from afar may just see something completely hidden to you.

WHAT'S IT LIKE TO BE ON THE OTHER SIDE OF YOU?

Ryan Leak is a top-rated keynote speaker from Dallas who has an amazing ability to inspire people to over-achieve. I've gotten to know Ryan quite well, and I look up to him as a mentor. One of the most important questions that Ryan asks his audiences is: "What's it like to be on the other side of YOU?"

What's it like to be your friend?
What's it like to be your co-worker?
What's it like to be your classmate?
What's it like to be your business partner?
What's it like to be your significant other?
What's it like to be the person interviewing you?

Each of us have blind spots and we need someone to tell us what we do that's wrong and what we can do to get better. Be prepared to take constructive criticism from another.

ACTION ITEM
Ask someone you're close to for some constructive criticism today.

THE TERM "MENTOR" WILL NEVER LEAVE YOUR VOCABULARY

Mentorship is such an important part of this journey. You'll not only have multiple mentors throughout your life, but you'll also become a mentor to many. The nicest part of mentorship is that no matter what side of the equation you find yourself on, you'll learn and grow from the experience. Someone sharing with you issues they're dealing with that require valued input will no doubt help you identify issues in your own life that will benefit from this thought process.

Mentorship has so many different looks. A recent YouTube video that reached viral status was of Golden State Warriors Head Coach Steve Kerr interacting with his star player Steph Curry. In this situation, Coach Kerr merely needed to validate to Curry what his stats reflected because the player was "in too deep." Steph was upset with what he viewed as subpar play, but his coach was able to look at the real stats and prove he was doing tremendously well.

Here lies the problem: So many of us don't take the time to step back and see our successes (or failures) from the outside. We're just too busy dealing with life and all it throws at us to make that ever-important reality check. This is why there's so much value in inviting that outsider (the mentor) into our lives for a fresh perspective. It doesn't matter if you're 22 or 62, that perspective is always welcome. Find it and use it. Often.

YOUR FIRST MENTOR WILL BE YOUR ULTIMATE GUIDING LIGHT

There is a common bond amongst the business leaders and sports icons I've worked with over the years: their committed interest in the success of our youth.

As I asked these professionals for their input on getting college seniors on track for this exciting next step in life, the importance of having a guiding light alongside for this process is the underlying thread shared by all.

Like those before you, you'll no doubt have many mentor figures in your life (I sure have!), but that first one—the one who will truly set you on your path to success—is the one whom you'll remember forever and the one whose tips for success you'll no doubt share with those leaning on you for advice.

ACTION ITEM
Make a list of potential mentors for yourself.

YOUR MENTOR MAY SEARCH YOU OUT

Olympic swimming champion Janet Evans won four gold medals in an Olympics career that spanned three Olympiads. Janet tells the story of a fateful meeting with swimming legend Mark Spitz at the site of her first Olympic Team's training session in Hawaii before the 1988 Seoul Games.

Mark Spitz had shown up at the pool specifically to meet Janet Evans. Spitz asked the 17-year-old phenom about her experience so far. Janet's response was that she had *finally* reached her lifelong goal of making the Olympic Team.

Mark Spitz knew that Janet Evans needed a mentor.

Spitz knew that Janet was much better than the low target that she'd set for herself. Getting to the Olympics allowed Janet to do so much more for herself and her country. He persuaded Janet to change her attitude, adjust her goals, and, in the process, transform herself from a winner into a Champion.

SOMEONE WILL TAKE A CHANCE ON YOU

I've introduced you in this chapter to keynote speaker Ryan Leak. I initially met Ryan because three of my customers in the same week told me that I needed to hear this special speaker whom I'd never heard of. And, oh, were they right.

Ryan grew up around the church. His dad was a pastor, and Ryan found his speaking skills by spending every weekend telling stories to his congregation.

When Ryan addresses corporate audiences, he always shares a Powerpoint slide that details how he got in front of this particular audience. From one of his early schoolteachers to his first employer to the person at church who realized Ryan should speak to the church, and, ultimately to *me*. This slide reveals the fact that someone will take a chance on you when you least expect it.

Ryan Leak had no idea that I was about to show up in his life.

YOUR MENTOR MAY ALREADY BE ROOTING YOU ON

A mentor becomes your champion in life: a trusted advisor. They're someone who knows you, believes in you, and inspires you to over-achieve your goals.

NBA Hall of Famer and Billionaire Businessman Magic Johnson is one of the most popular motivational speakers in America. He tells a story of his need to find a mentor in business once he knew his NBA career was coming to an end. All Magic had to do was turn to those fans sitting in the courtside seats (media moguls, movie stars, business executives, etc.) who'd been rooting him on at Lakers games all those years. Almost everyone he reached out to was there to have a meeting with Magic, give him advice, and get him started on his new career.

Your mentor is sitting in *your* courtside seats: a family friend, your coach, one of your professors, or even a regular customer at the Starbucks where you work. Once you show an interest, you'll be amazed at how many people are eager to help you.

ACTION ITEM
Make a list of five people you can ask for help. Then ask them for help!

A MENTOR'S FEEDBACK IS INVALUABLE

Your peer's thoughts, or your mentor's feedback, on that last interview will certainly give you great insight into what went right and what may have gone wrong. Before sending that follow-up note to that prospective employer with whom you just met, bounce the note off someone you trust.

Sometimes we're all in this too deep to be able to stand back and get a good perspective on how we're doing—or what we're doing.

Feedback from those you trust is key.

BE PREPARED TO SHARE YOUR EXPERIENCES

All it takes is a few smart moves to get yourself going—and others will notice. Trust me on this: Many of your fellow graduates are already sharing their initial success stories with those currently in college looking for the stars. Be prepared to share what you've learned with others. It will inspire and motivate people you don't even know.

AIM FOR THE STARS WHEN SEARCHING FOR GUIDANCE

It may seem that reaching out to the CEO of a startup is a bad place to start—even if you somehow have that person's email address. It's widely known that Mark Cuban responds to any and all emails that come his way, so the answer is always YES, send that email and reach for the stars.

But the key here is just what you say in this email. Merely asking Mark Cuban for advice, or a job, won't heed an immediate response, but sharing with him an understanding of his business dealings and successes over the years—and how that's inspired you on your path to success—just may.

YOUR BEST MENTOR MAY BE IN THE CLASSROOM WITH YOU RIGHT NOW

We've discussed how even the most successful people in business today have mentors in their lives. It's so important for you to understand that this is more than a single person's undertaking. I know that you may want to go at this alone and do it your way as a learning experience with its ups and downs and failures and rejections. And trust me, that's going to happen, and we'll have you prepared for that. But this is not intended to take you away from that path. You need a trusted advisor on board to guide you and bounce ideas off. This certainly could be a group of strangers you meet on Reddit, but you'll soon find that one of your best mentor targets is likely one of your professors.

Not only do your professors see you every day in class and around campus, but they'll know your work ethic and they're there to help. Your teachers are some of the best cheerleaders you have, and one of their biggest advantages to you in this process is just how connected they likely are. A professor is an amazing link to the real world out there. They have friends and key contacts in a multitude of industries. Many college professors today are former corporate executives, or in the case of adjunct professors, are currently employed by companies big and small.

This is not about getting an A in this class. It's about developing a team of trusted advisors excited to help push you along in this process. Why search outside of your comfort zone if this cheerleader is in the game with you already?

When a professor posts office hours, be the first to stop in. Doesn't have to be for a lengthy discussion on this week's class: This is about you, or rather, it's about your professor. Remember, people love to talk about themselves. Give this person every opportunity to tell you how they got to this point in their life. They'll open up to you and will want to know the same about you and your goals. When it comes time to apply for jobs, this person will prove to be a lot more to you than just a great reference letter.

ACTION ITEM
Identify a professor who fits this category and take the time to invite them into your network.

REMEMBER

In HELP, we learned to delegate a key duty in this process to a learned resource: a mentor. Mentors have valuable insight to the journey you're about to take because there are parts of this road they've driven on many times before.

Be a good listener, ask a lot of questions, but go with your gut. Because after all is said and done, this is *your* success process and not anyone else's.

LET'S DO COFFEE

It's simple. It's real. And it's going to make this process work for you. It's a coffee meeting.

The key here is the request for a coffee meeting. Or should I say the *continual* requests. Because this is a part of the process that you should enjoy for your entire career. I truly thrive on coffee meetings.

Don't wait for an interview at your target company to pop up on a hiring platform or on Reddit. Get a meeting with someone at that company on your own today and on *your* schedule.

Effectively this is meeting with someone to *not* talk about business or your career. It's as simple as that.

A coffee meeting is an informal get together for a brief period with someone you'd like to meet to develop a relationship with and further build your network. Remember, this person will *not* have a job opportunity to fill, but you shouldn't be surprised if the outcome shifts. Your target list for these meetings will consist of people you've identified as those whose advice you seek. And the request is a simple message on LinkedIn: "I'm looking for some advice and would like to hear more about what drives you to succeed. May I buy you a cup of coffee sometime soon?"

This invitation needs to go out to an extensive list but understand that only a select few will respond.

THE COFFEE CODE

Why will some respond, though? Because a few short years ago, they were in the same boat as you.

During the coffee meeting (to which you are the first to arrive), you are in query mode. Remember, people love to talk about themselves. Let that happen here. You need to have done your homework on this person and on their company beforehand. Have questions in mind to ask: *How'd you end up here at Google? Was this something you wanted to do when you were in college? What are some of the pros and cons of working there?*

Your hope is that the subject of this meeting turns to you. And if it does, then you save a question like this: *What do you feel that I should be doing to get on a similar path as yours?*

But you have no say in this decision to make this meeting about you, so you need to show off your people skills in the meantime. Be courteous. Be a great listener. Be genuinely interested in what this person has to say. Be respectful of their time with you. Try your best to subtly interject why you would be an incredible asset at their company. I do know that this final suggestion goes against the thought of "this is *not* about you," but I have found in life that if you don't ask for something, you don't have a shot at getting it.

So, unlike an interview—which is a set meeting for a specific role for a set period of time in an office setting where the next candidate is sitting outside the room just waiting for you to fail—this coffee partner of yours could just leave Starbucks and go back to their office and absolutely rave to the team about you and try to grab you before someone else does. So, you may just have turned this coffee meeting into an interview. Or…you can ask them for a referral.

Maybe this newly found fan of yours can suggest someone at their company or another whom you should meet to talk about an actual job at this company. By asking for a referral, you've elevated yourself from a "do me a favor and let's meet for coffee" relationship into a prospective employee with instant credibility because of this referral.

You cannot let up after just one successful coffee meeting. It needs to be in your arsenal of ways to get meetings at any company.

This may be hard to comprehend, but your goal for coffee meetings is not to get a job; it's to create Raving Fans of yourself. Once you've created that fan base, you need to consistently stay in touch with each and every one of these contacts because you never know who's going to reach out tomorrow to hear more.

But this doesn't mean ignoring the old-fashioned way of getting interviews. Sometimes this may be the only way that a company representative will meet with you. Those interviews will be set meetings for specific openings at a company. And even though you may not feel "qualified" for a specific role, apply for that interview. You may dazzle an interviewer to the point that they may actually find another job for you at their company.

ACTION ITEM

Identify one company of extreme interest to you. Use LinkedIn to find three employees in roles you feel are meaningful to your career path. Reach out to them.

THE MAGIC OF MEETING PEOPLE: HOW MAGIC JOHNSON ACTUALLY BEGAN TO BUILD HIS NETWORK OF CONTACTS, THEN USED THAT SAVVY TO MAKE A HUGE DEAL

In the previous chapter, I shared how Magic Johnson had a courtside network of raving fans to pick from in his search for a business mentor. What Magic actually did when he retired from The Lakers was reach out to the ticket office manager at The Forum (the Lakers' arena at the time) and ask for a list of all of the names and addresses of those season ticket holders who had courtside seats.

Magic WROTE HANDWRITTEN NOTES to each of these individuals; half of them responded, and two of them are still Magic's business partners on some of his billion-dollar deals today. The notes were simple, along the lines of "Can we meet in your office so I can pick your brain about business?"

True, this was Magic Johnson. Who wouldn't want to respond favorably to this request? Well, you might be surprised that half of those Magic asked for meetings didn't respond. So, if that's your lesson in the art of continually reaching out to people, let that be it.

Once Magic began his business career, he realized the importance of shooting for the stars, trying to accomplish the impossible. Case in point: a meeting with Howard Schultz, founder of Starbucks.

Magic knew that Howard Schultz had never sold an individual Starbucks store, and he had no interest in franchising, but Magic had a creative idea that he *had* to get in front of Mr. Schultz. The fact was that Magic understood the inner-city communities all too well, and he knew that people living in lower-income communities would spend $5 on a cup of coffee just like those in upscale areas. Magic just had to find a way to convince Schultz of this reality. After a series of boardroom meetings in Starbucks' Seattle offices that led nowhere, Magic realized he had to change his strategy and get Howard here to LA. Magic invited the CEO to one of the movie theaters he owned in LA.

It was the opening night of *Waiting to Exhale*, starring Whitney Houston. The theater was packed. As Magic shared, "Our biggest screen had 500 women inside. Suddenly, every woman thought she knew Whitney Houston personally and started talking to the screen. So, Howard grabs me about 20 minutes in and says, 'Earvin, I never had a movie-going experience quite like this.'"

Magic explained, "Guess what happened? That got me the deal."

Magic built 125 of his own Starbucks stores in urban America. And it put Magic on the map for his business savvy. Look how adding a personal touch can get you a deal.

ACTION ITEM
It doesn't have to be an invite to a movie theater you own to make an impact. Write down three ways you can add a personal touch when you reach out to someone. Then try them out! The worst that can happen is that someone will ignore you—exactly like what happened to Magic.

NETWORKING 101, GARY VEE STYLE

As we watch social media superstars gain millions of followers each day, it sure appears that the one with the most TikTok views or Instagram followers wins. But to win in your game, you just need the *right* connections.

You need to put yourself in a position to meet people, either in person or online, and this needs to be an ongoing process (even if you truly feel that you already have enough connections or that you've achieved what you set out to do).

Gary Vaynerchuk is one of the most influential entrepreneurs on the planet, thanks in part to the social media platforms that he dominates. Yet, when asked about the value of face-to-face networking to build your brand equity and connections, Gary goes all-in. He tells young people the importance of creating an environment around yourself that showcases you, your strengths, and your passions. Engaging face to face with as many people as possible is the key. Ask a lot of questions, but don't assume people will ask you questions.

But if you find yourself at a Networking Event, Gary suggests you do *not* find the most influential person at that event and latch onto them. Because if you do, chances are great that you may miss meeting the one person who was going to make all your dreams come true.

MAKING NEW CONNECTIONS IS A PRIORITY

This is the story of a 27-year-old law school graduate who needed direction in his life. Once I understood the value of relationships, there was no stopping me on this journey. Let's start building relationships for you as I have for myself.

OPPORTUNITY + PREPARATION = LUCK

Pascal Finette is the Chair for Entrepreneurship at Singularity University Think Tank in San Jose, CA. Pascal's advice as you prepare for the next step is a lesson in "strong vs. weak connections."

The strong connections are people like yourself. It's easy for you to connect with them because you see them at school. They're like-minded to you.

The weak connections are those unlike you. These are people with different interests and backgrounds. When you connect with these people, they'll open whole new worlds for you because they'll show you things you've never seen before.

Pascal shares, "So, go out there and make friends, make connections, and remember what Roman Philosopher Seneca said over 2,000 years ago: 'Luck is what happens when preparation meets opportunity.'"

Be ready when luck hits you.

JUST GETTING AN INTERVIEW IS HUGE

The day that you set up your LinkedIn account was the day you proved to yourself that you're ready to meet people and make connections in the business world. Interviews, coffee meetings, talking to someone in line at a movie who works for a company that interests you, these will all yield terrific connections that you may not use today, but you sure may use tomorrow. Keeping in touch with these people on a regular basis is key.

As you enter this interview phase of the process, you'll soon realize that the more people you try to reach, the higher your percentage of replies. You'll also find your creativity skills being tested in this quest for a handshake, as there are many others out there vying for that same meeting with this same person.

Whether it's a five-minute meeting, a 30-minute question and answer session, or a half day exam-interview, value every one of these opportunities that only you have created.

The mere fact that you've been granted an interview should be viewed as a huge win. And once you've got this one under your belt, others will follow.

Be prepared to listen well in any new environment. *Something* that this person says will no doubt have extreme value to you, and you don't want to miss it.

JUST WHOSE JOB SEARCH IS THIS, ANYWAY?

I see so many job applicants get nervous, stressed out, upset, and frustrated over job interviews. But it really doesn't have to be this way. While you are certainly trying to win over this interviewer by reciting all the things that you think they want to hear, there *is* another side to this equation because this job search is about what *you* want first and foremost, and *not* about them.

THE MORE PEOPLE YOU MEET, THE MORE YOU'LL BECOME THE FOCUS FOR OTHERS WANTING TO WORK THIS PROCESS

Here's the reality of the journey on which you're about to embark: As you meet more contacts and take on these amazing roles with companies that interest you, you yourself will become the one who's targeted by others looking to start this process. It's a never-ending cycle! But the fact is that you'll *want* to share what you've learned with others—just as I have. And if you have a job—for instance, as a Production Assistant with Sony Pictures—you'll no doubt have made contacts in the film industry along the way who may be of keen interest to others eager to get a foot in the door.

Be prepared to share your pathway to your current success with others.

MAKING CONTACT: THE SIX DEGREES OF SEPARATION RULE

As you embark on building out this network of yours, you'll no doubt reach out to your dad's contacts. And your mom's. And your friend's mom. And your neighbors. And your teachers. Let's make the toughest part of this road trip be the thank-you notes you send out to those whose offers of employment you *didn't* accept. Because if you play this part of the game right, you'll have lots of opportunities.

With the understanding that there's very possibly no set course to the exact position in life that you'd like to attain, your role now is to search far and wide for friends, acquaintances, and contacts you've made at internships and part-time jobs to ask them to be a part of your network. You've heard about that Six Degrees of Separation principle, right? It's the theory that *anyone on the planet can be connected to any other person on the planet through a chain of acquaintances that has no more than five intermediaries.*

I'm here to tell you that this number is closer to two or three. It's tremendously likely that somebody you know—or rather, somebody who believes in you—has a contact with 72 and Sunny, Dropbox, Deloitte, The NBA, ABC News, Google, Edelman, Wasserman Media Group, Pixar, Ralph Lauren, and even Bill Gates. It doesn't matter the industry you'd like to get into; you do have a contact or friend who knows someone in that industry. It's your job to identify areas of interest to you and then just ask. Because if you don't ask, you'll never get it.

MAKING YOUR OWN BUSINESS CONTACTS USING LINKEDIN AND OF COURSE, COFFEE!

Derek is a recent graduate of Boston College who successfully used LinkedIn and coffee meetings to get himself a "reach" job in Hollywood.

The reach job was any role associated with a Hollywood studio, a TV show, or a movie production team. The problem was that Derek had no contacts whatsoever in the film or TV industry. His family was from Cleveland, and he had just spent the last four years of his life in Boston.

Derek took to LinkedIn and searched for film and television executives with similar backgrounds to his. Hollywood types who'd graduated from Boston College, or from any school in Boston, were targets, as were the same who came from Cleveland. Once Derek identified the favorite few, he went to work. Since the simple Connection Request on LinkedIn limited Derek's abilities to type longer than a few sentences, he opted for LinkedIn's Sales Navigator, which allowed him to send messages of any length to these potential connections. The message was an invite to coffee, but Derek tailored each message to that specific person and their company and their role at that company: "I'm a recent graduate of Boston College with an extreme interest in the film and television industry. May I buy you a cup of coffee to hear more about how you ended up in your current role and hopefully get some advice as I begin my career?"

Derek immediately landed coffee meetings at major talent agencies, production companies, and studios. His first job was as a Production Assistant at CBS on *The Talk*, and his continued eagerness to land a studio role quickly led to an Executive Assistant role for a Vice President at Warner Bros. In just a few short years, Derek has now positioned himself as an executive with HappyNest, a startup animation production company.

Derek's hack for the *why* of getting as many coffee meetings as you can, especially here in LA: *In a town like this, the cool jobs never get posted.*

BUILDING BUSINESS RELATIONSHIPS FROM A NAVY SEAL'S PERSPECTIVE

One of my company's motivational speakers is a former Navy Seal who served on the same Seal teams as famed heroes Marcus Luttrell, Rorke Denver, and Chris Kyle. We recently discussed the Sales process—specifically how *everyone* is a salesperson, no matter your age or your occupation. What I learned from that talk reinforced my belief that persistence does pay off. Here's what he shared:

"Whether you are trying to get an interview for a new job, reaching out to a production company for a role on a production crew, interviewing potential investors for your startup, or cold-calling potential buyers of a product or service that you're offering, your job is that of Relationship Builder. To build a relationship with someone, you need to get to know them. And you need to learn the best way to add value to their interests, to their families, and to their business.

Relationship Building in business is a five-step process that does not happen overnight:

- A STRANGER becomes an

- ACQUAINTANCE, who becomes a

- FRIEND who becomes an

- ALLY who eventually becomes a

- BUSINESS ASSOCIATE.

Does every attempt at building a business relationship work? No way. You will get turned down all the time. But the more you throw out there, even more will come back to you. The key is to reach your fullest potential at whatever stage you're at in this game—and then get ready to do it again but better, smarter, and stronger."

A SIMPLE HANDSHAKE CARRIES A LOT OF WEIGHT

This is all about relationships. Last year, I traveled with Magic Johnson to a speaking engagement in Nashville so that I could shake hands with that customer of ours who'd booked the event. I'd only spoken to this person on the phone prior to this meeting. I knew that soon after this engagement with Magic, this company would have another need for my services, and I made it a point to stay in touch with this relationship I'd made to ensure that the call wouldn't go to a competitor of mine. (Hint: Be proactive in the marketing of yourself and your brand.)

ACTION ITEM
Identify some business relationships you've made where you can go "deeper." Then take that next step.

SPREAD OUT YOUR CONTACT REQUESTS

I was at a lunch meeting recently with a customer discussing his family when he told me how he gets inundated with calls, letters, emails, and LinkedIn requests from prospective suppliers asking for his business. He says that sometimes these people interact with him so often with information that he didn't request that he simply says, "Please unsubscribe me."

The balance between requesting and pestering is often hard to understand.

ACTION ITEM
Make a spreadsheet detailing your contact reach-outs and requests. Make it a point not to reach out too much.

REACH THEM THE OLD-FASHIONED WAY

Go back to the phone. Emails may seem to be the way of the world, but the personal touch of a phone call will always keep you in position A. And don't ever forget about the story of Magic Johnson and the way he handwrote personal notes to each of the Lakers fans sitting in the courtside seats.

EVERYBODY ASKS FOR FAVORS

The more parents I talk to, the more I hear, "Our neighbor knows the anchor on Channel 2 News and they can get Brian an interview at the station."

It's amazing to me just how many strings are pulled and favors requested each and every day. And so many of them are just to get jobs like the ones you're eyeing or applying for right now.

You need to accept the fact that there *will* be strings pulled by parents or friends of those trying to get in the same company as you. But you can't let that get you down. Maybe there's no open spots at this place—or maybe there's ten. And the process itself may take a long time. So, keep asking for the favor.

MEET WITH A MENTOR —AND WORK THEIR NETWORK

Based on the fact that a mentor can be anyone who shows interest in helping you reach your goals, these LinkedIn coffee partners, parent's friends, professors, and more will all have *their own networks* that you'll need to tap into. The real question becomes: How bad do you want this?

This process will take a lot of time and effort on your part. Ask for referrals. Take notes. Keep files. Track leads. And be prepared to meet many new people along the way.

Every single person you are about to meet with has gone through this same exercise more than once. That's why they're about to help you.

LET CONNECTING ON LINKEDIN BE ON YOUR WEEKEND TO-DO LIST

I begin each day in my business as if it's truly a new day, as though I'm starting my business from day one. On the weekends, I reach out to potential new LinkedIn connections in hopes of hearing from them on Monday with a brand new opportunity. And yes, while that may appear a bit blind-sided because of the many other connections and leads and customers I've established over the last few years, I've always found that my business—like yours—is an absolute game of numbers. The more people you reach out to, the luckier you get. And if you're not sure about reaching out to a specific individual at that company, do it anyway! Remember though to consistently let your current connections know what you're up to.

REFERRALS: YOUR RAVING FANS

I started my business with one client: Lakers Coach Pat Riley. My goal was to make Pat a wanted commodity on the lecture circuit. How'd I do it?

One deal at a time.

Pat spoke to Sears, and I focused my marketing on the standing ovation he got for that company. People talked, word got out, and then I got another speech for Pat with Bayer Pharmaceuticals. As I let the world know how Pat did for Sears *and* Bayer, he gained more and more fans of himself as a speaker. And as his popularity grew, so did my business.

In this equation though, Pat Riley is *you*. And you're a master at self-promoting. When you leave a meeting or an interview or just a handshake with the person you've just sat next to on a plane or in a shared Uber, leave a lasting impression. Create raving fans for yourself. People will remember you, and they *will* tell others. Just be prepared for the resulting calls.

BE A GOOD LISTENER

The more people you meet and the more you put yourself out there, you'll find that people who've been in your exact position seriously want to help you.

During any meeting, be a good listener. Sure, they want to hear from you. But when that interviewer speaks, perk up and hear every word. You may just hear the best way to land a job at this company.

YOUR NEXT JOB IS IN THE HANDS OF A FRIEND

Many of the assistants we hire here in our office are part-timers fresh out of college or grad school. The only problem with offering someone part-time work is that they're still out there looking for a full-time job. Why is that a problem? Because everyone eventually finds that full-time job. It's all a matter of looking in the right pool.

Take Kelsey for example. A recent marketing grad from Tulane University, Kelsey came here to LA to get into the fashion and design industry. She came on board with us after having sent her resume out to 200 companies, which led to two decent prospects, but no offers. Then Kelsey reached out to a friend who'd just gotten a job in the fashion world who hooked her up with a soft interview. Kelsey knew this was just an exploratory meeting and didn't bother to even bring her resume along.

She walked out of that meeting with an offer.

You need to realize the breadth of your current contacts. Someone you know with the same interests as you may better understand how to find that perfect job. And that's a lot easier than the process of going through the motions of submitting resumes everywhere.

PROPERLY CONNECTING ON LINKEDIN

The point of LinkedIn requests is to connect with people. You can't merely find 100 potential contacts on LinkedIn and click *connect, connect, connect, connect* with me. You need to take the time to draft a very short note (because you're only given a certain number of characters to personalize an invite).

That being said, there is tremendous value in signing up for LinkedIn Sales Navigator. I was at a convention of hotel salespeople recently, and a LinkedIn expert explained the fact that you can use Sales Navigator to pinpoint key people at target companies to reach. And using that deeper platform, you can actually write a message that has NO length limitations.

Yes, it may be a bit more expensive, but you are here to play the game. Make sure that you're addressing this individual by first name and talking about their company and a specific role that you can tell they relate to.

YOUR NEXT INTERVIEW MAY BENEFIT A FRIEND

In the process of you being a good listener during an interview, you may learn something that can help a friend. You're interviewing for a Business Strategy Ops assistant position at Dropbox, and you find that they're looking to hire a new creative associate on their Culture team. Your roommate just spent the summer interning with Ritz Carlton Hotels as an assistant to their Culture Coordinator, and they would be a perfect candidate.

Without you being at that first interview, this potential opportunity never would have surfaced.

Always be prepared to help a friend to reach their goals. Not only will they do the same for you someday, but also your abilities as a judge of people will consistently be enhanced. That's just one of those gifts you have that will work to further your career development.

YOUR CLASSMATES: FRIENDS IN THE CLASSROOM BUT COMPETITION FOR A JOB?

Let's look at those people you see each day on your school campus. They're in your classes, on your teams, and in your study groups. Many of them are going to be interviewing for the same jobs you're trying to land.

Are these people your friends at school but stabbing you in the back at the next interview?

No way.

Many future business relationships are made in schools just like yours. Your best friend may come up with an idea for the next big startup, but *you* have the know-how to get it up and running. Or your teammate's idea for a startup needs a financial mind, and *you're* an accounting major.

How about your classmate in the middle of their interview at an Ad Agency who realizes that the best person for this job is *you*? Your friendships on campus could just be the beginning of business partnerships for life.

IT'S NEVER GOING TO BE ABOUT YOU, BUT REMIND THEM ABOUT YOU

When you get the chance for a phone interview, a live interview, or the preferred coffee meeting, remember that in the process of building a relationship that this is not just about you.

Be the first to ask questions of the person you're meeting with. Not just about how long they've been with this company and what had led them to working there initially, but about their family and a fun city they may have recently visited. Share your interests. If you have a love of food and restaurants, ask them about their favorite eats in your city. And show that you truly care about their responses. When you send a personal note or email as a follow-up to this meeting, make sure and say something that relates to this important conversation. This person will appreciate the reminder of who you are and will respect the fact you sent this note. Beyond a mere handshake, these are the difference-makers in the building of a relationship.

STAYING IN TOUCH: LINKEDIN AND THE LEAKY BUCKET THEORY

Thanks to an ever-expanding world of technology, you're thriving in an amazing era of connectivity. You may not realize the enviable position you're in right now with your advanced knowledge and access to so many social media platforms which give you the ability to interact with virtually anyone. Companies, not just individuals, have their own social accounts. And these aren't just for fun; this is how they get customers and do business.

I have a friend who's a realtor for a major real estate company. Her company suggests that they interact with their key customers 33 times a year, be it by phone, text, email, shaking hands, and through every possible social media platform. The reason for these interactions is The Leaky Bucket Theory.

The Leaky Bucket Theory is the idea that if all your customers are inside a big bucket that's filling up, the more customers you gather will cause some to leak out. It's a theory about retaining customers, but it applies to you because of all the new contacts you're about to make. These new people you're meeting need to be interacted with often. You've no doubt made an impression on these new connections of yours, and if they can't help you today, they'll be there for you tomorrow. You just need to keep them in the loop so they don't fall out of your bucket.

THAT PERSON NEXT TO YOU ON THE PLANE

You never know who you're sitting next to, so yes, you talk to that person on the plane. Most big company executives fly coach, so there's a chance that the person in 16C may just have some influence on your future. A professional sitting next to a 20-something on a plane will no doubt want to know where you went to school, what you studied, and what your future plans are. Why? Maybe their company has found value in recruiting on airplanes!

My son was a computer science major at Boston College. He suggested to me that he'd considered flying roundtrip from here in Los Angeles to San Francisco or San Jose each week in hopes of sitting next to someone at Google, Dropbox, or Yahoo. That may just be a good gamble.

Every business person or student I've met on an airplane is on LinkedIn.

LET OTHERS AT THIS COMPANY KNOW YOU'RE INTERVIEWING THERE

You've been trying to land an interview at Google for the last year. You've made contacts there through LinkedIn and through friends, but nothing turned into a meeting. You even shook hands with a Google exec at a recent job fair. You really want this one.

Then, through Google's website, you get an interview. It may not be for the exact position you've dreamed of, but it's Google. One of the key preparations you must make for this meeting is to reach out to those people at Google with whom you've had contact along the way and let them know when you're going to be there. Watch how your persistence pays off.

THIS WORLD IS A LOT SMALLER THAN YOU THINK

Once you're in a position within a specific industry of interest to you, you'll soon find out what a small world this really is. All those studios here in LA may seem to be fierce competitors, but if you look at the resumes of employees at these companies, it's just a back-and-forth switch from one production company to the next.

So, it seems that everyone does know everyone else. But once you can get yourself into this loop of connectivity, you'll start to see some amazing business opportunities that fall within reach on your road to success.

REVISIT YOUR LIST OF CONTACTS OFTEN

Meeting your new network of business contacts took time, preparation, creativity, guts, hard work, and even luck. These people will never forget you as long as you regularly interact with them.

They may not have helped you when you thought you needed them, but they'll be there to help when you really do.

ACTION ITEM
Add a new contact to your network each week.

CONNECTION REQUEST: YOUR BUSINESS FRIENDS WHO HAVE YOUNG KIDS

Picture this: You're a highly paid corporate executive at a major advertising agency. You have three kids in college. What emails start to load up your inbox around January or February? Emails from friends of your three kids and their parents or business associates of yours who have college senior kids who would do anything for a meeting with you or someone at your agency.

Here's a great tip I figured out. Let's say you have an in with an executive at a key company. Now, let's say that person has kids, but they're *young* children (not in college, but in middle school). This exec does *not* have that loaded inbox in February with all those requests because they don't run in those circles just yet (no 12-year-old cares about a job interview). You've just identified your target.

ACTION ITEM
Name at least one friend who fits this profile.

REMEMBER

In MEET, we saw the value of a Coffee Meeting and how this is so much better on so many levels than an interview.

We better understood how LinkedIn can be used as a networking tool, not just when you meet someone to add to your network, but also to stay in touch with that person on a regular basis. We now know the importance of keeping our eyes and ears open anywhere and anytime, and how networking can take place in areas you'd least expect.

CHAPTER FIVE:
WORK CONSISTENTLY *PERFECT* YOUR PLAN

There's no set path on this road to → ⋰SUCCESS⋱

THE POWER OF NICE
THIS TICKET WILL HELP YOU GAIN ACCESS ANYWHERE

"Shoot for the moon with big dreams and be persistent."
— BEN NEMTIN

YOUR VOICE **MATTERS!**
— ADAM GRANT

Develop a **PLAN** + WORK THE PLAN

OVERWHELMED?
- Change your priorities
- Take a break

PREPARE FOR A **YES**

BE **PROACTIVE**
ASK for what you WANT.

BE *comfortable* WITH BEING **UNCOMFORTABLE**

ADAM GRANT'S INSIGHT: YOUR EXPERIENCE COUNTS

You may not have a lot of experience just yet, but your input and ideas have tremendous value in the workplace.

Adam Grant is one of the most famous organizational psychologists in America today and Wharton's top-rated professor. He's the author of multiple *New York Times* bestsellers, including *Option B* (coauthored with Sheryl Sandberg) on building resilience and finding joy in life.

Adam studies companies to figure out what makes one organization successful while another may fail. His insights to success are based on real data, and he's a hugely popular speaker and thought leader.

During a recent keynote for one of our customers in the residential mortgage industry, Adam shared a story about the value of a new hire's opinions at even the most powerful companies. He'd studied Bridgewater—the world's largest hedge fund—and its 1,500 employees. Young business school grads line up for a chance at an interview with Bridgewater, and Adam found out why: New hires at Bridgewater are invited to agree or disagree with the business principles that the firm was founded on 50 years ago. If a suggestion makes sense based on this feedback, Bridgewater will revise their principles. These actions from the top of the hierarchy show us that

1) you have a voice right from the start, and 2) senior leaders don't always have the right answer.

Other companies, just like Bridgewater, are continually listening to fresh ideas from young minds like yours. Be prepared to be a voice of reason in any organization. Your ideas do matter.

YOUR PLAN HAS MEANING

Nothing can happen in life without a plan in place. It can be brief, or it can be in-depth. But once you develop that plan and set it in motion, there's nothing to stop you from succeeding.

I've been a salesman working for myself for 30 years. I never worked for a big company. My dad had his own business selling disposable medical supplies to hospitals; it was an offshoot of his father's business. I'll bet that had my dad worked for a large company that I'd have done the same. But I have no regrets. What's important here to note is that whether you work for yourself, for a small company, or for a huge conglomerate, the game's the same.

My grandfather used to wear a suit and tie to work every day and he had a tie clip that he wouldn't walk out of the house without. People today still wear tie clips, but this one was engraved with eight simple letters: YCDBSOYA. My dad continued to wear these same tie clips every day he went to the office. And he'd always remind us what YCDBSOYA stood for: *You Can't Do Business Sitting On Your Ass.* Some things never change.

My dad also carried a briefcase to work every day. He had a saying engraved on that briefcase: *Develop the plan. Work the plan.*

These were the two credos that he lived by every single day as he made cold calls and built a future for our family.

DEVELOP A PLAN AND DON'T LET UP

Everything is sales. I'm sure you've heard this many times, but whether you're looking to raise money, pitching a creative idea, trying to get a job or hire someone, you are in sales mode. And without a plan in place, you can't make a move.

The "plan" here is a full understanding of your product, idea, target customers, competition, and whatever it is that you're preparing to sell.

A salesperson who knowns their product inside and out can only succeed.

ACTION ITEM
Develop a short plan right now for your latest goal.

BEN NEMTIN'S PLAN

At the lowest point in his life, bestselling author and influencer Ben Nemtin made the decision to only surround himself with people that inspired him. That one small decision completely changed his life. After creating *The Buried Life* for MTV, with the realization that so many of the things that Ben and his friends truly wanted to do in their lives were essentially buried by work, school, and life, Ben was able to create the most epic bucket list of all time. That mission took on a life of its own, gaining raving fans along the way. Items checked off that list included writing a *New York Times* bestseller, having a conversation with Oprah, playing basketball with President Obama at The White House, and having a beer with Prince Harry.

However, the most powerful piece of this bucket list project was Ben's desire to give back to those who couldn't fulfill their own bucket lists. THIS is the world you want to create. As Ben shares, "When you take this next journey, whatever you do, just know that there will be ups and there will be downs. There will be times when you will struggle. We are told to be strong, get through it on your own, and don't be someone's problem. But the truth is—from someone who has been there—this is backwards. We are all human beings. And when you hit that struggle, know this: you are not alone. More importantly, asking for help in that time of need comes with no shame. Because whoever you go to for help will one day return the favor and come to you in their time of need. This is the world we want to create. A world of connectedness and compassion."

Ben Nemtin shares that as you ponder your next moves in life, know that the goal you have—even if it seems impossible—is possible. But you need to take the reins and do it. And you need to stop and think about what is important to you. It's easy to put those dreams on hold and get buried by the everyday grind. Shoot for the moon with big dreams and be persistent. Success depends on consistency of effort.

THE BUSINESS PLAN YOU DEVELOP TODAY WILL LOOK TOTALLY DIFFERENT TOMORROW

If you believe in something, stick with it. It could be a short-term project or a long-term idea. Give that project all the time it takes to develop it, shape it, massage it, and get a result you're proud of.

Do not let up.

That project will never look the same as it did when you first came up with it. Every day you'll learn something new and add it to the mix.

WHAT'S YOUR U.S.P.?

We all have a Unique Selling Proposition, and you need to know yours before pitching an idea or going into *any* meeting.

Remember when Danny Meyer asked me "Why You?" That was not Danny asking me to find my brand or my strength; that was a request for me to look deep and figure out what I am doing here. What can I add to this conversation and why should I be heard? These are the questions you need to ask yourself.

MARK CUBAN ON TALENT

Mark Cuban is a true identifier of talent. He likes to prepare young people for success in any field of interest. One of my favorite things Mark Cuban has ever said is, "Whatever industry you pick, if you outwork everybody, if you try to be a little smarter than everybody, if you try to be a better salesperson than everybody, if you try to be better prepared than everybody, you've got your best chance. Because if you *don't* do it, somebody else will."

ONE CEO'S PERSPECTIVE: CHANGE ISN'T ALWAYS THE ANSWER

Randy Garutti is the former CEO of the popular hamburger chain Shake Shack. Randy shares a story that he was first told by his mentor from college.

Randy had lived in seven or eight cities in the first eight years of his career, and he kept jumping around from one job to the next. At that moment, he had decided to move to New York City from Seattle. His mentor said, "You're too young and stupid to appreciate this today, but someday you'll tell this story. When real learning happens, it happens when you stay. It happens not when you jump from the next thing to the next thing to the next thing. That's not learning. Learning happens when you are sitting in the same seat and you see the seasons change around you. That's when learning happens."

Randy moved to New York City, and 20 years later, he's still there, having had multiple roles in the same seat with the best learning he's ever had.

THE POWER OF NICE

I've stepped back and looked at the people I've befriended, the places I've gone, the amazing events that I've attended, the memorable things I've been able to do over the years, and I realize that so many of these opportunities were afforded me simply because I'm a nice person.

Nice can get you anywhere you want to go. It helps you start a conversation on an airplane, at a sporting event, in line getting coffee, in class, at an interview, or at work.

Nice people tend to float to the top. They get noticed by professors, employers, co-workers, or by an executive with whom you interact at your part-time job. Employers like nice people because they get along with everyone in the office (these people tend to be the *glue* that keeps everyone together). Business associates tend to open up to those they feel comfortable speaking with, and that's a quality of nice.

Nice will ensure you an enjoyable life ahead. It's not worth discussing the flip side.

IT'S JUST A MIDTERM

Ever take the time to count the number of final exams you've taken in college? Now, think about the number of midterms you've taken leading up to those finals.

If I asked you which type of exam you've had more practice with, the answer would no doubt be a midterm. What was the difference between a midterm and a final? There was less information to study, so the midterm likely didn't require all-nighter study sessions. You didn't have to close your life out to all your friends and fun activities. Once you received your grade on a midterm, you knew the areas you needed to focus on, and you got a good feel for how you were doing in the big scheme of things. And if you failed a midterm, the world didn't end. I'll bet you got right back up and tried again. You tried until you succeeded.

Welcome to the real world. It's just a midterm. But along the way, you're going to learn some exciting things about where you fit and how you can make a difference.

ON THE JOB

You've made it. You may have 15 jobs before you're through. I've been in the same business for over 30 years, and I'll bet your parents are close to the same. For you, the business world's about to become your buffet.

So now, it's all about your attitude, your work ethic, your passion, and your desire to find the perfect fit for your needs. You may take a job in a large office setting and realize you should be running your own business. But you never would've seen that until you went through this process.

Wake up early and get to work prepared to make a difference.

THINK LIKE A REASONABLE PERSON

Even though I've made my share of mistakes post-law school, the key principle I learned in those three years sticks with me still today: Be a reasonable person in everything you do.

A trial judge uses a "reasonable person test" when deciding the outcome of a case: What would a reasonable person with ordinary prudence do in this same situation?

Whether you're making a split-second decision or a long-term determination, stop for a moment and understand your options. Weigh those options from an unbiased standpoint. And then make a reasonable choice.

The time you spend to stop and think will be worth its weight in gold.

ACTION ITEM
Are you about to make a key decision that may require a bit more thought or input from those around you? If so, take a moment to think.

OFFER VALUE

I learned long ago not to reach out to a lead or a customer without offering something new of value to them. I like to refer to this as a deliverable. This isn't a Starbucks gift card, but it's information that's new to this contact.

Don't touch base with an email that says: *Any new Production Assistant openings there at Sony Pictures Studios since we last met?*

Instead, you want to write a note that says something like this: *I've just finished a three-month program as a freelance script reader at CAA and I'd love to see if anything new has opened up for a Production Assistant role at Sony Pictures Studios.*

STARTING OVER EACH DAY: THE MENTALITY IT TAKES TO BE A TRUE ENTREPRENEUR

When you have your own business—as I have for over 30 years—you don't have a paycheck coming each month unless you earn that paycheck. There are no guarantees other than the fact that you're the boss, and the harder you work, the luckier you'll get. And the fact is that the bills have no reason to stop each month, so you've gotta work hard.

Competition?

Oh, it's there, but you cannot have your competitors in your periphery. Once you start looking for your competition, you lose sight of number one. Know that your competition is there but leave it at that. Obviously, when you set out to start your own business, you'll learn a heck of a lot about the competition in your space. You'll know what they do right and what you feel they do wrong, and you'll figure out how to enter this industry using your creativity and insights to do it a little bit differently and a whole lot better.

ANY field you choose will have competition; you just need to be prepared to work smarter, stronger, and more creatively and efficiently than others to get the job done.

Your hard work will be noticed. Trust me.

But here are the facts: Once you get started, you cannot let up. Success breeds competition. That's to say that once you become successful in the space that you've chosen, others will hear of your

THE COFFEE CODE

success. And while some may be proud of you, others will want to join in on this piece of the pie that you've so nicely sliced out for yourself. You need to be ready for this.

Every single day that I have a win in my business (and by *win* I mean make a successful deal), I have effectively grabbed this business from a competitor. Obviously, there will be those clients who become loyal to you and your brand, but a win of any size in business is a tremendous accomplishment.

THERE'S NO SET PATH ON THIS ROAD TO SUCCESS

Here in Los Angeles, if you ask five people how to get to Disneyland, you'll hear five different sets of directions. I just wish success were as easy a destination to find as Disneyland is.

Your drive to success will take you down one-way streets, through alleys, and into cul-de-sacs. You may just find your way onto a freeway or two. You'll hit rush-hour traffic, road closures, and detours.

A friend of yours driving to the very same destination may arrive hours before you or days later.

But you will *both* arrive.

THE MADNESS OF MARCH

I know it's tough to realize that others much older than you are going through this same process right now. From a job searching standpoint, no national event highlights the value of adding to your resume like a coach in the NCAA Basketball Tournament tries to do each year.

March Madness focuses on the top 68 college basketball teams in the country vying for the title of National Champion. But if you're a coach for one of those 68 teams, each one of your nationally televised games during March Madness puts you on a national pedestal in front of any college program looking to upgrade their current coaching roster. And it's not just the head coach in the spotlight; other schools realize that your assistant coaches are just as responsible for not only building the success of this current team, but also preparing them for today's opponent.

Sometimes, in this tournament, you only have to win one single breakout game to draw attention to yourself and to your staff of assistant coaches. Treat each day like you're trying to win a National Championship game.

You will get noticed.

TODAY MAY BE A STEP BACKWARDS

On a roll, and all of a sudden something takes you back to square one?

The time you just spent to get to that strong position *was* NOT wasted. Pick yourself up and realize you're in a much better place today than you were yesterday.

To me, the game Chutes and Ladders is the ultimate microcosm of your process right now.

Life's a big gamble. It consists of constant rolls of the dice. You set a goal, and you hope to attain it. You'll make it to the top of the ladder only to suffer a setback that may slide you back down even below the point at which you started.

The STRONG ones—all of you—will get up, wipe yourselves off, and try to get to the top again. But the difference between Chutes and Ladders and your personal game is that in real life, you will LEARN from each of these experiences that knocked you down so that you'll not walk that same path again.

WHAT A PERFECT TIME IT IS RIGHT NOW

As you begin this exciting career journey, you won't realize it, but you have more time on your hands now than you'll ever have. Let's maximize this available time today.

YOUR CHARITABLE ASSUMPTION: DON'T ASSUME THE WORST OUTCOME BECAUSE THE BEST IS JUST AROUND THE CORNER

Too many of us brace for the worst. It's not fair to yourself, especially since you work so darn hard to prepare for meetings and interviews. Assume the best will come to you, even if that result is a bit delayed.

A charitable mindset assumes the best intentions of others.

Always be ready to apply a charitable assumption to any situation where you're hoping for a particular outcome but are worried that things may have changed for the worse. Even though you may be number one in your mind, you're not necessarily number one in the eyes of another who's about to respond or react to you because other projects have taken priority for them.

I deal with this every single day in my business. I put a proposal in front of a customer, and I don't hear back from them. Another day goes by and no response. And I'd been told before our initial meeting that time was of the essence, and they were on a deadline to get this deal done. Deadlines in business tend to fly out the door because other deadlines come in and take precedence. You just have to be prepared for other deadlines to step on the importance of yours.

PREPARE FOR A YES

Be prepared for that positive response from one of your connections. Know the next step before you even get there.

Ever watch the pros play tennis?

It's not about the first shot, but it's all in the way a point is set up. Rafael Nadal is able to react to his opponent's shot better because he knows exactly where that next shot is going to land. You need to set your tactics up in the same way: anticipate a response and know what directions you need to turn next.

ACTION ITEM
Review one of your current leads. Assume that person says YES. What will your next move be?

WANT SOMETHING? IF YOU DON'T GRAB IT, SOMEONE ELSE WILL

Proactive. This word needs to become a part of your daily routine. Want to achieve the best results for yourself? Those results won't come to you unless you go and get them. Never assume that someone will call you or track you down, even if you have a sure thing. Always be prepared to take that extra step and make that extra call or send that extra email.

And always leave asking a question: How can I get your business? What's it going to take for you to invest in this idea of mine? What can I do to secure this job you're offering? If you don't ask, you'll never get it.

ACTION ITEM
Write a question today that you can ask during your next meeting or interview.

DO ONE THING AT A TIME AND DO IT WELL

If you feel like you must do 100 things today because you're being rushed, STOP. Slow down and prioritize. We ALL feel this way very often, and you are not alone. Do things at your own pace. The important things will make the top of your list and will get done first. If you can't get to something on that list, then it's going to get done some other time or it's just not going to get done.

You can only do the best you can do.

We all try to be perfectionists, and that's admirable. But the more projects you take on, the more people you meet, the more opportunities you learn about, and the fact is that you can't do them all. I'm not saying that you can't do them all *well*; I'm telling you that you cannot do them all. And that's okay.

ACTION ITEM
Grab your list today and delete one item from "Must-Do-Now."

POSITIVITY WINS EVERY TIME

Sometimes the toughest days are the ones where you wake up and think the world is going against you. You feel like you can't win, no matter how hard you try, and that each step you take in a positive direction gets wiped out by backward steps.

We all deal with this at every level of life. Sometimes it's really hard to realize that this will pass—especially when you're right in the middle of the tornado—but this is when you truly need to stay super strong and know that you'll get through this one.

Sadly, there will be more instances in your life like this. But amazingly, there will be exponentially more of those amazing days when everything just clicks into place.

This process is a combination of good and bad. Dealing with the bad with a positive attitude is going to help you approach each day with your head up.

DON'T GET OVERWHELMED IN THE MOMENT

We've all woken up in the middle of the night worrying about what's to come.

Know that everybody has this same issue. Your plan will see itself through. Even if that plan is not yet written in ink.

CARE LESS ABOUT THE COMPETITION

I've taught my kids to employ the same sales strategy that I use in my business every day: *Know* that the competition is out there, but assume *you* are going to get the business. Once you stand back and look at the stark reality that there are thousands of others out there doing the same thing you're doing—and even applying for the exact same jobs—you're sunk. Do not sink your own ship. Be creative, be personable, be passionate about this opportunity, be nice. But *want it* and *ask for it*.

THERE'S NO WRONG STEPS

Face it, your course will change. That's a good thing. Just remember that ANY job you take—ANY step you take—is the right step.

There are no wrong steps out there in the real world.

BE EXCITED TO LEARN

You learn something new every day.
    If I didn't say this today, I sure thought about it.

You think you know it all, but you're not even close. Every new situation you come across will be a learning experience. And this new knowledge will no doubt help you today or sometime later in life. Keep an open mind and be willing to learn.

IT'S NOT JUST YOU

These same processes, the same issues, the same emotional roller coasters that are taking control of your life right now are being dealt with by everybody else around you.

Keep your focus, and don't stop working the process.

BE COMFORTABLE WITH BEING UNCOMFORTABLE

You need to accept the fact that we all have ambitious goals. We all want to be the President of Disney, but we need to start at the bottom to get through the process. And being at the bottom is not a comfortable position.

You'll no doubt see friends and others make quick jumps toward these goals, but just remember that there's room at the top for everyone.

DON'T BITE OFF MORE THAN YOU CAN CHEW AT WORK

In my business, there are absolutely times when I'm in the weeds. And then the phone rings or a new email shows up in my inbox, and I *must* answer it because it may just be a new piece of business.

Four important points:

1. Understand that *everybody* is busy. Most people I deal with are so impressed that I try to always answer my phone or respond immediately to every email.

2. If you're in your own business and you're generating responses that you cannot handle, you need to reevaluate your business plan and hire help.

3. If responding to a new opportunity potentially puts you in a stressful place, respond when you're in a calmer situation.

4. If you *must* respond, be prepared to prioritize your list every single day.

WE CAUSE OUR OWN STRESSES

You're probably worrying about things right now that aren't even in your control. Likely, the things that stress you out most are self-induced. Direct your energy at what you *can* control. And don't let the little things take over your life.

You took on four projects when you knew you only had time for two. You canceled on one lunch meeting because you felt that a different lunch partner would help your career more. If you'd plugged in your phone earlier, it wouldn't be at 4% right now. If you hadn't gone out last night, you'd be better prepared for today's interview.

You've got to stop sometimes—a lot of times—and stand back and look at the big picture. Not enough of us do this. Too often we live life in the moment. It's so very important to enjoy the ride.

YOU'RE NOT EXPECTED TO BE A KNOW-IT-ALL

You're young and learning. Soon you'll realize, if you haven't already, that you'll *always* be learning. But for now, the curve of learning may seem a bit cumbersome.

Accept each new opportunity that's put on your desk as a challenge. Prioritize it. Ask questions. Figure it out. Get through it. Grow with it.

The more inquisitive you become, the better the chance that you'll uncover the next step to your success.

PREPARE TO BE A SELF-STARTER

Your school projects were many times team efforts: you'd take on a role geared to your strengths and others would have different tasks. In the real world, there may not be another team member to rely on.

Whatever role you find yourself in, you need to be super-prepared to be organized in every aspect of the process. And you need to assume that the only person you can rely on is yourself: drafting a business plan, making files, reaching out to contacts, taking notes, and tracking leads. Every single day may be something new, but in the beginning, at least, you may only have yourself to talk business with. In the process, you'll find new ways to validate your own successes.

BE A LEADER, NOT A FOLLOWER

Baseball's famed Dodgers Manager Tommy Lasorda once told me that there are three types of people in this world:

- The ones who make it happen.
- The ones who watch it happen.
- The ones who ask, *"What happened?"*

Be the one who makes it happen.

BE HAPPY, BE REALLY HAPPY, WITH WHAT YOU'VE GOT

So many of us (myself included) are on the constant lookout for the next best thing. And there are so many platforms surrounding you now with those next best things.

But is that the right way to go about this game?

I don't think enough of us realize just what it is to have great choices in life. Tuning out may be the best choice for you.

Step back, take a look at your life, and be genuinely happy with what you've got. That next opportunity will show itself. I'll bet you won't even have to search it out.

BECOME A MASTER INTERVIEWEE

Interviewing may be viewed as a process, but you need to walk into THIS interview with the goal of landing THIS job. Don't make it a process if it doesn't have to be one.

My daughter moved to New York City after graduating college and set off to get a job. Thirty interviews later, she had become a professional interviewee with no job. Had she approached the process wrong? No.

Getting a job isn't easy. But your attitude as soon as you walk in that door is key. There's tremendous value in the interview process. You gain a level of comfort and a lowered-stress level with each new meeting. You learn more about yourself, and you become a better listener who gains an understanding of what these interviewers want to hear.

Once you've got a couple of interviews under your belt, this engine of yours is about to become a well-oiled machine. The interview process does not happen overnight, so there will be times of drought, wondering, worrying, and reevaluating to come. Just know that it's happening. You're figuring out the formula to getting multiple job offers.

ASK FOR THE JOB

I often find myself in the company of decision-makers in my daily quest to make as many deals as I can in my business. Getting the ear of a decision-maker (a business contact or an interviewer for you) is the result of being a terrific go-getter who truly wants to get the job done.

I've found one thing to be certain in those meetings: I *must* ask for their business. If I don't, I've wasted a golden opportunity to advance myself.

You only get one chance to make a first impression.

Don't be just another interview subject coming in for the 2:15PM slot. Stand out. Tell them you want this job. Why not give *them* an action item: **What's it going to take for me to earn this job?**

ACTION ITEM
Prepare a list of questions for your next interviewer.

SEEMS LIKE NOBODY'S LISTENING? THEY ARE

There will certainly be a tendency during the process to feel like nobody's listening to you, that you're the best-kept secret around and nobody cares. Don't worry, they'll notice.

In a meeting or an interview, people will take mental notes about you as well as physical notes.

Online, people will review your LinkedIn page without you noticing.

In offices where you've interviewed, your resume will be circulated to people you never imagined would see it.

And all of the people you've been impressing in the meantime won't soon forget you.

TAKE TIME FOR A BREAK

I recall that I never took a break when studying for the Bar Exam. I felt guilty going to a movie or a game or just taking off a Saturday afternoon.

That was wrong.

Sporting events, shopping trips, movies, plays, comedy clubs, museums, farmer's markets, and more are wonderful diversions that'll give you a chance to clear your mind and maybe even come up with a creative idea to better market yourself.

Getting to the gym for a scheduled workout is key, not only to stay in shape, but also to feel better about yourself.

This is all about self-care. Self-care means taking the time to do things in your life that help you live better and continually improve both your mental and physical health.

Self-care can help you to manage stress, lower your risk of illness, and increase your physical energy.

ACTION ITEM
Set this book down right now and go do something for your well-being. The book will be waiting for you when you return.

STAY FOCUSED

As this game of life progresses, there may be a tendency to lose track of why you're here. In the Kentucky Derby, the greatest thoroughbreds in the world wear blinders around their eyes to keep them focused on the prize and not on the peripheral opponent.

As we've discussed, there will be many speed bumps along the way that will try to prevent you from achieving your ultimate focus. Do not be deterred. Good things take time.

HOW'D YOU GET THAT JOB?

If you were to research ten new hires at any large company, you'd likely hear ten different stories of how they ended up getting that job.

It's not all about those job fairs at your school, and you don't necessarily have to be an intern first. Some got there through connections at that company, some by coffee meetings, some went through the interview process, and some may have been a combination of everything. But trust me, they didn't all get on a bus and get dropped off at that company.

Just because your path may look different from those who've gone before you doesn't mean you won't get there.

LUCK

I've always found that the more calls I make, the luckier I get. It's all a game of percentages. If you had all the time in the world to get your resume out to *everybody*, you'd have a ton of offers. But we don't have that kind of time, so we must pick those potential jobs of interest that show open positions or try our luck and go after companies that we want to work for but that don't necessarily have current openings. The latter is tougher, but if you're creative, persistent, and you've done your homework on a specific company and position, you'll no doubt shine.

ONCE YOU'VE PIQUED THEIR INTEREST, DON'T LET IT GO

You're busting your tail to try and get a return email or phone call or a cup of coffee with a key player at a company in your top ten. You got that meeting, but your contact has rescheduled three times.

Do not wait a week to wonder if they're going to call you back. The longer you wait, the closer to the bottom of their pile you'll fall. Once you've made it to the top of someone's list, do all you can to stay there. Nobody's going to get mad at you for trying to grab something that's right there.

NOT MANY CALL-BACKS? SEND OUT MORE RESUMES

You're trying to enter a fast-paced business world on the ground floor. This is like getting on a freeway from a dead stop. It's hard to find that opening. Prospective employers and business associates not responding to your emails or calling you back? Don't take this personally. They're busy and just like you, they need to prioritize their lives each day. Try looking at it this way:

DISCOURAGEMENT = MOTIVATION

Everything is about timing. You cannot get discouraged if you don't hear back from a group of prospective employers that you reached out to.

If they're not looking now, or if they're too busy, or if something else is on their plate that's more important, you're just not going to be seen and you need to tee it up again sometime in the near future.

ACTION ITEM
Minimize this obstacle by making more calls to prospects.

BE OPEN TO ANY OPPORTUNITY

Since any road you choose can lead to your success, always be open to anything that comes your way, even if you see absolutely no tie-in to your career path. A job at a local restaurant will enhance your people skills. A job in sales of ANY type will enhance your negotiating skills. If you want to get into the Hollywood scene, any opportunity to work on a film as an extra, at a talent agency doing assistant jobs, or any studio role will be huge.

ACTION ITEM
Review the job you're interested in right now and find some roles that may be more entry-level or that have lesser requirements. Set your sights a bit lower and see what happens.

PLAY THIS WORLD LIKE IT'S YOUR WORLD

Don't worry about what others are doing out there. There's only one person that you can completely control. Make your world a microcosm of the real world. Build *your* experiences, *your* dreams, *your* moments, and *your* successes. Don't wait to see what everyone else is doing or building or buying. Do it your own way. They'll catch up to you.

THERE'S NO RUSH TO DO WHAT YOU LOVE

Worried that going to grad school will take three more years of your life? Scared that you may be 27 years old and still not know what you want to do with your future?

You're not alone. Your personal happiness comes first.

I learned long ago that nobody cares whether you're 24 or 34. When I was 27, I was a production associate for NBC Sports, working weekends at NFL, MLB, and College Basketball games. It sure didn't matter to me that I was a law school graduate at the time. I was doing what I loved.

TAKE ADVANTAGE OF EVERY BUSINESS OPPORTUNITY TO HONE YOUR SKILLS AND IMPRESS OTHERS

My son Ryan had a wonderful job as a Technical Director at Dreamworks Animation here in LA. However, he recently left that job in pursuit of his own software startup. His partner in this startup, Thomas, was a freshman who dropped out during his first year at Georgia Tech.

Thomas had a three-month internship with Samsung while he was a freshman, and he shared with me the fact that every single day was an amazing learning experience that made him feel proud to come to work. But as Thomas got more involved in projects at Samsung, executives and others began to take notice of this brilliant young mind working for a limited time on their team. During those three months, Thomas was able to learn from the best and hone his skills. He worked hard and people noticed him, so much so that he was recruited heavily by Samsung to work for them full time. He refers to the internship as "a three-month interview."

You never know what opportunity may be *your* "three-month interview."

NO TIME YOU SPEND IS WASTED

So, you're on a roll with great callbacks and new interest, and then everything goes sour.

What do you do next?

The time that you spent to get to that strong position was NOT wasted. You've just made some terrific contacts for the future, and you've likely developed a "deck" on yourself, or your startup, that you can now adjust for the next opportunity.

YOU'RE BETTER OFF TODAY THAN YOU WERE YESTERDAY

Every day in life is a learning experience and another chance to grow. You may not realize it, but your brand today is so much stronger than it was yesterday, last week, last month, and last year.

THE WORD PROACTIVE

This word needs to become a part of your daily routine. You may be the best candidate, have the best idea, have developed the best brand, or have built the best startup out there, but unless you're proactive and let people know about it, you'll just have the best-kept secret in the world.

ACTION ITEM
What's one thing you could do TODAY to make more people aware of you?

ACCEPT PRAISE, BUT NEVER EXPECT IT

Many of us need praise or thanks to stay motivated. But the time spent waiting for it sometimes won't be worth your while. I truly feel that we are in a thankless world. A lot of people just assume that you'll take on a project that was delegated to you and see it through to the finish. Those people have zero interest in thanking you for a job well done. When this happens, you should not take it personally. Accept praise when it's offered to you, but never expect it. You know you've performed well; when the crowd cheers, you'll already be on to the next one.

YOU'RE ONLY A COUPLE OF DEALS AWAY FROM TRUE SUCCESS

I'm a small business owner. So, I'm not always afforded some of the benefits of working for a big company—most notably, a regular paycheck.

When you work for a paycheck based solely on your sales productivity, you'll sometimes find a roller-coaster pattern in your income that's directly related to the deals you make. Being put in that scenario makes one key life lesson very evident: You're only a couple of deals away from true success. It's the inspiration behind the constant need of a salesperson to land that really big account.

The best example of a "deal" is a real estate agent selling a house. Depending on the size of that commission, one or two deals can take you to an entirely new level in this game.

What this basically means is that there's such a fine line between our thinking of what success should look like and what failing looks like. And that fine line is all subjective. Your fine line looks different from mine. If you've set what success needs to look like in your world, you'll constantly strive for that success. Understand that over your lifetime that look of success will change many times. From a basic need standpoint, that look means paying your current bills. It's not getting ahead; it's getting by.

So, let's examine "getting by" as our basis for success.

If all you can do is get by paying your basic expenses each

month, that doesn't mean your life is stagnant for one second. It means you're building a foundation with somewhat of a regular income. Too many of us think that we need to build this entire city by ourselves overnight. That's just not the case. There's something to be said for the success of just getting by—even though in reality, you're not just getting by, you're enjoying a wonderful level of success and enhancing that success every single day.

We also put lots of self-imposed stress on our lives based on what others are doing. But sometimes, you need to look at the success of others as motivation for you to strive to be a little bit better. Because the difference between that level of success that someone is sharing on Instagram and the level where you are is only a couple of deals away.

YOUR SUCCESS WILL AFFORD YOU TIME

We've looked at what can happen when one or two deals take you to a new level of success. Now that deal doesn't have to take place overnight; it can be a single real estate sale, or it can be a wonderful long-term job opportunity with an employer from your bucket list. But what you'll see happening after making that deal is that you put yourself in a cushy position of no worries for a period of time. You've effectively bought time to decide on your next move, relax, or focus on the job at hand. The bottom line is that success many times can afford you time. And time has tremendous value. So, enjoy it.

LEAVE YOUR MARK

What if you weren't at this job? Or better put, what if this was one of the job offers you turned down? Would this job have been done more effectively had you not been there? You may never know.

That said, it's true that nobody has the identical goals, creative mindset, and skillset that you do. An organization that misses out on you will still have its successes; they'll just get there in a different way with a similar set of team members.

We all approach things differently. Our creative minds may all have similar goals, but they get there in different ways. What *you* bring to the party will be of keen importance to the organization you join. They expect and need you to prove your value to them. That's why it's important for you to leave your mark in any role you choose.

You've been very successful up to now. Continue to do things your way. That's why they'll hire you. And that's what they'll miss most about you when you leave for job number two.

WAKE UP EARLY

I get my best work done early in the morning. In the morning, prospects answer the phone and return emails.

Why?

Because I'm the only one calling and emailing them.

Get up early and start before everyone else. You'll be amazed at just how much you can do when nobody's around.

IT'S YOUR FIRST JOB AND MORE WILL FOLLOW

I had the entrepreneurial spirit on steroids when I started my business. I got out of law school, took a desk in the rear of my dad's office, and started making cold calls in an industry I knew nothing about.

Quickly, I learned that the more calls you made, the luckier you got.

Many of your peers today, with that same idea of starting their own business, take a different approach. They accept jobs in a field that interests them, and they gain as much knowledge as they can before setting out on their own.

There are so many valuable learning experiences to be had in your first few years in the workforce, and you'll find that many of them repeat themselves. Once you've mastered the learning curve in a particular industry, new opportunities will no doubt arise.

Don't stress if your first job isn't everything you dreamed of.

FIND YOUR ZONE AND STAY THERE FOR A WHILE

I'm sure you've met your share of friends from well-to-do or highly motivated families who are currently worried to death about getting that high-paying first job out of college at JPMorgan Chase.

Some graduate to five-star jobs. Others grab part-time jobs, assistant roles, and positions at the bottom of the ladder. But the dream is the same.

The path that you choose to your dream may be 180 degrees different from someone else's path. Stay on your course at *your* speed and watch how success will find you.

AM I AT THIS JOB JUST PREPPING FOR THE NEXT?

No. The next opportunity you get will show its face big and bold. Don't just go through the motions at a job knowing that it's your springboard to the next job. That's not fair to you, and it's certainly not fair to your employer.

Give all you've got at any opportunity you choose. Be proud to work there and show them that you care. You may not realize it immediately, but the experience will pay off for you in the long run.

THE RIGHT TIME IS RIGHT NOW

Don't ever feel that you missed a deadline or missed out on an opportunity to apply for something special. Timing may be everything, but that amazing opportunity will always resurface. And once it does, you'll be in an even better position to get it.

ACTION ITEM
What have you missed out on lately that you now need to revisit?

CHOOSE YOUR WORDS WISELY

Whether you're sending an email or meeting someone face to face at a business meeting or a cocktail reception, the words you use are so very important.

Take the time to *think* before you say something. And sometimes, staying silent may be the best move.

THE ONLY THING YOU CAN COUNT ON IS CHANGE

Change is inevitable. You wake up early and fight traffic for an early morning meeting with a potential employer. Five minutes before the meeting, you get a call that they've just cancelled. The *next* time you meet this person, just watch, you'll end up with a longer meeting with a more attentive audience. I've learned to always use change to my advantage.

Too many of us overreact to change. Get creative and figure out a way to incorporate this new set of circumstances into your life.

IF YOU'RE HERE TO PLAY THE GAME, PLAY IT WELL

Once you find a job, there's no reason to ever let up on your persistence. There will always be new opportunities making their way to you, whether you searched them out or they found you. Be open to moving on to a new chapter, but if the time isn't perfect right now, your next break will be waiting.

REACH FOR UNATTAINABLE GOALS

We're all motivated to succeed at different levels. Success to me is much different from success to you. If we succeeded at everything we tried, there'd be fewer challenges out there. So, we must constantly challenge ourselves and set new goals.

Set those goals high. You're not going to win every time, but you'll be consistently inspired to get there.

IF LIFE MAKES YOU TURN DIRECTIONS, GO WITH THE FLOW

You may find yourself on a roll and then a family emergency changes your priorities. You'll find a couple of things will happen. One, you'll be back after this issue is taken care of and it will be like you never missed a beat. And two, since you've already set the wheels in motion, you'll no doubt continue to get looks and calls and interest based on your earlier work, since the only person who knows that you may have changed directions for a minute is you.

STAY ONE STEP AHEAD OF THE COMPETITION

Even though your classmates may not be your competition in the fierce job market out there, there *will* be competitors. And I'm certain you'll know who they are.

Whatever position you find yourself in, know your competition and what they're up to. That knowledge will keep you in a position to stay ahead of them. Don't let the competition get the upper hand. This is *your* game.

YOU AND I DO THE SAME EXACT THING

I'm a salesman. Every day I wake up to a list of people that I send emails to, asking for their business. I attach links to references, a website, and anything else that will convey my value and establish credibility. I'm hoping that one or more people on this list will respond in the affirmative that they are interested.

Sound familiar?

I'm doing EXACTLY what you're doing as you look for a job. And yes, the keys of hard work, perseverance, not taking no for an answer, and more all come into play.

In one way or another, everyone needs to sell.

HAVE A WINNING ATTITUDE; IT'S CONTAGIOUS

Your winning attitude will make others better. Take your team along for the ride of their lives.

COMPETITION DOESN'T ALWAYS HAVE AN UGLY FACE

You're about to be exposed to many different personalities, office politics, co-workers who don't get along with anyone, and competitors in your industry. Just because someone is a competitor of yours doesn't mean they're your enemy. Yale Professor Barry Nalebuff (the founder of Honest Tea) calls this competitive friendliness "co-opetition." It's the understanding that opposite forces many times can get together to form a common bond.

REMEMBER

In the WORK chapter, we used insights from influencers, including Adam Grant and Mark Cuban, to help us realize that your hard work *will* get you noticed.

We saw the importance of having a plan in place and sticking to that plan by waking up early and staying late. But even a perfectly laid-out plan will change direction when you least expect it. In short, the only constant that you can count on is change. Lastly, we understood to never wait for thanks for a job well done. Remember: Accept praise, but don't expect it.

CHAPTER SIX:
FAIL — LEARN FROM YOUR Losses

"NO" means "NOT RIGHT NOW"
— JENNY FLEISS of RENT THE RUNWAY

LIFE TAKES OFF on the other side OF FEAR
— NFL HALL of FAMER TONY GONZALEZ

There's ALWAYS another way in the DOOR

your options are LIMITLESS

TURN:
NO → YES
REJECTION → ACCEPTANCE
Discouragement → Motivation

REJECTION is REDIRECTION!

NO DOES NOT NECESSARILY MEAN NO
— MARC RANDOLPH, CO-FOUNDER of NETFLIX

YOU MAY BE THE PERFECT FIT AND THEY JUST DON'T SEE IT. MOVE ON.

Your successes in life got you to this point... ...There's LOTS more to come!

NO NEVER MEANS NO

The story to instill this idea in you comes from an entrepreneur named Marc Randolph. In 1997, Marc co-founded Netflix with its current executive chairman Reed Hastings. Marc learned never to take no for an answer when he was a senior at Hamilton College in upstate New York. A large advertising agency had come to campus to recruit for an account executive role. Marc applied for the role and passed the initial interview; they then flew him down to New York City for the follow-up meetings at the next level. Eventually, Marc made it to the final rounds of interviews—competing with three other candidates. After a full day of stellar interviews and meetings with what felt like half of the firm, Marc was told he didn't get the job.

Disappointed, Marc took action. He thought to himself, "What am I missing?" So, he wrote letters to every single person he had met at that firm and asked them what he should do differently next time.

The response to those letters was another invitation to come back to New York City, and after a brief meeting, Marc ended up getting the job. How? Turns out the firm hadn't offered the job to *any* of the four finalists. They just wanted to see which one wouldn't take no for an answer. It's a lesson learned that Marc Randolph preaches to any young person he meets: In a business context, *no* does not necessarily mean *no*.

REJECTION IS JUST A PART OF THIS GAME

Jenny Fleiss is a popular entrepreneur and speaker on resilience and failure.

Jenny was in Harvard Business School when her roommate's sister Becky purchased a $2,000 dress for a gala thinking that she may meet her future husband there. For a millennial in debt with a closet full of clothes, this purchase was a tough one for Becky. With so many online photo platforms used by Becky and her peers to share what they've worn at parties and weddings, the likelihood that this dress—or any of the other dresses in her closet—would ever make its way outside again was minimal to say the least.

Jenny's business idea: Build an inventory of designer dresses to rent to women for single-event usage that can be returned and traded for another dress at any time. A subscription service they called Rent the Runway was born. They tested the idea with some Harvard undergrads and a "This rocks!" response from one student after trying on a gold sequin dress was all Jenny needed to see the power that fashion had to restore confidence and empowerment to a woman.

Jenny and her roommate first brought their concept to Diane Von Furstenberg—one of the most famous clothing designers in America. Diane shared with them all the reasons why she hated their idea. This gave these women even more motivation to succeed.

But the toughest part of starting this business was getting outside dress design companies (Ralph Lauren, Dior, Tory Burch, etc.) on board so that Rent the Runway could market their dresses. Jenny had an average of ten meetings per designer, with older male executives who didn't understand the millennial mindset and who couldn't fathom why this idea would be a hit. For Jenny, every *no* was an opportunity to learn. And she took this mindset a bit further. She didn't interpret a no as a *no*, instead she viewed it as *not right now*.

Rent the Runway has gone on to employ over 1,000 people and Jenny's estimated fortune of tens of millions of dollars has given her the ability to now develop ideas in new fields of interest.

THE REJECTIONS THAT LED TO THE BEGINNING OF MY BUSINESS

Before I started my company, I was a law school graduate with a cool part-time job with NBC Sports as a production associate. My role was to write and prepare the graphics for weekend NFL and College Basketball games and then work gameday in the production trucks outside the stadium, sitting side by side with the director and producer of that live event. I wanted nothing more than a full-time position with NBC Sports, and I was more than willing to move to New York City to realize that dream.

After every game I worked in the trucks, I'd send a handwritten note to the producer and director with whom I'd just been onsite. I thanked them for the opportunity and let them know that I wanted to be a full-time employee if they heard of any openings. I was trying my best to set myself up for success.

Whenever I got word of an opening, I jumped at the chance. But even with all the experience I had, and all the great relationships I'd made, it just wasn't to be. I regrouped, and that's when I started my own business doing what I still do today.

FAILURE IS AN OPTION

If you were to study some of the most successful businesspeople in America today, you'd find a myriad of stories about failure. Failure to many is the ultimate motivation to get the next one. Should you fail, you'll understand this statement.

THE ONLY PERSON WHO CARES ABOUT YOU IS YOU

When the pandemic hit and turned our world upside down, it eerily reminded many of us of the adverse business effects resulting from the 2008-2009 recession. Businesses shut down and dreams were lost.

Adversity has many faces, and you will no doubt see a societal impact again on your journey. But the fact is that you can never fully prepare for an event of this magnitude—especially knowing how it may affect your friends or business associates—so having some level of self-sufficiency will always help you to handle the worst.

SOMEONE WILL TAKE A CHANCE ON YOU, MAKE THEM PROUD OF THAT CHOICE

At some point, *all of us* are unqualified, but there is going to be something about your attitude, your background, your personality, or your level of confidence that will pique the interest of someone looking to hire you or partner with you. Someone will take a chance on you. Expect that chance to come every single opportunity you get.

THE WORD "NO" IS YOUR FRIEND

Too many of us hear the word no and just stop or slow down. The key with hearing no isn't as much the word itself as it is what got you to the point of hearing that response. Why were you told no—or better yet, how'd you get in a position of hearing no in the first place?

You likely identified someone in a decision-making capacity who took the time to not only review what you had sent them but also to respond to you.

THAT'S HUGE.

So many of your peers don't even get the chance to have their emails read—and there's no way to know if your email was seen. I've heard stories of corporate executives with thousands of unopened emails.

Let's think about this and what it means. First, an executive isn't about to reject you if they never even read your email. So, don't ever feel that a lack of response is the same as being rejected. Next, even if it doesn't feel like the right thing to do, send another email to a non-responsive person after a reasonable period of time. I don't know what reasonable looks like here because everyone is different. You just have to go with your gut feeling on this one.

The fact that an executive may not open all of their emails means one thing to me: You need to consistently interact with as many potential contacts as you can. Throw a ton of darts at that dartboard. And once you think you've exhausted that list, find more names and send more. Someone will read your email and respond. But should they respond with a no, you need to find out *why not.*

Why not could be an issue of timing. Maybe they just hired someone in that role. If that's the case, you need to ask if there are other people within their organization that you should be targeting, or better yet, when should you next reach out to this contact (since this person now knows who you are).

The no could mean that these people just don't need the services that you're offering. But a follow up email right now while you have that person's attention is key.

A bunch of nos will soon equal a yes. And then a second and third yes. And then you'll get a feel for what a yes looks and feels like.

POST-INTERVIEW

Getting a callback, especially when you felt that meeting was one of the best ones in the history of meetings, has probably the closest connection to the sales process that I deal with in my business every day. The subjective nature of the follow-up is the most puzzling piece of this entire process. You don't know how much follow-up is too much and how little inquiring is not enough. When it comes to reaching back out to those you've just made a hopeful terrific impression on, the last thing you want to do is become the bothersome prospect.

But you may not get a callback. So, be prepared for rejection even though you know that you're the best person for this position. If they don't see that now, maybe they will later. Set up more interviews as soon as you leave this one.

Remember, these interviewers are new additions to your contact list, whether you got the job or not. Keep yourself on their radar. Follow up with a thank-you note and make sure they know where you ended up in this process. Your paths will cross again, I assure you.

YOUR OPTIONS ARE LIMITLESS

All of those people you're trying to get in front of right now have one thing in common: *They wish they were in your shoes.*

Look at the leaders of business today—so many are young people fresh out of school. You're armed right now with some of the best technology, best tools, and cutting-edge ideas to lead business to the next level. And trust me, those who are interviewing you know this.

Your options are immeasurable. So, don't even worry if you don't get that opportunity you thought you deserved.

THERE'S NO REASON TO DWELL ON THE PAST

If you feel that you messed something up in an interview, forgot to say something when you met a key contact for coffee, or said what you believe to be the wrong thing in one of these meetings, the only person who will notice this omission is *you*. Move on quickly. Nobody noticed.

MISTAKES ARE JUST A PART OF THE LEARNING PROCESS

As you strive for perfection, you will make mistakes, lots of them. They happen and everyone learns. You're not about to lose a job over a mistake. Dust yourself off and get back at it.

NO SUCH THING AS AN OVERNIGHT SUCCESS

Frustrated by no responses?

It's just a lull in the system reminding you to prepare for the storm.

You've heard the saying: *When the going gets tough, the tough get going.*

There will be times when things slow down for you and almost come to a halt. You'll think that nobody's calling you back and you've chosen the wrong direction.

How do you regroup in this situation?

I've found the answer is to never panic. You need to use this time to get better organized for the onslaught of activity that's about to come your way.

There are many times in my business when I'm close to making five or even ten new deals and I only get one of them. Knowing that I can be close on so many opportunities gives me the motivation to go out and find more, because sometimes the difference between getting that deal and losing that deal can be as thin as a thread.

BE AN AMBASSADOR OF GOODWILL

You'll often get rejected in this process, but enough will come back to you to make it all worthwhile. This is how you grow in life.

What you learn from rejection will be valuable for not only you, but also for your friends going through the same process.

Reach your fullest potential at whatever stage you're at in the game and give back your acquired knowledge to others.

LIFE TAKES OFF ON THE OTHER SIDE OF FEAR

NFL Hall of Famer Tony Gonzalez was one of the NFL's most dominant tight ends ever, but his road to success wasn't without setbacks. Now, he's a part of the NFL on Fox broadcasting crew. As he shares in his motivational speeches, Tony's dominance in sports and life was activated by fear. At a recent keynote for two thousand Dick's Sporting Goods Store Managers, I wrote down three key pieces of inspiring advice from Tony Gonzalez:

1. If you're serious about success, there are always going to be hardships.

2. Keep putting yourself in uncomfortable situations.

3. Life takes off on the other side of fear.

WHY AREN'T THEY CALLING ME BACK? RE-CHECK YOUR AIM

Let's say you're about to graduate from Northwestern and move to New York City to pursue your dream of becoming a TV writer. You've reached out to Northwestern grad Seth Meyers every which way you can think of short of becoming a stalker. The result?

Nothing.

You've figured out Seth's production assistant's name on LinkedIn and you've tried your magic that way.

Still nothing.

Now, you're frustrated and so upset you want to pursue a different career.

Stop it.

You think *you're* busy?

If it's the entertainment field you want to join, you're attempting to reach some of the busiest people on the planet. And those you are approaching have to-do lists that are 12 pages long, they've hired four assistants to help themselves get through those lists, and they personally don't even see most of those items.

Oh, you're on the list, trust me. But it's one of those list entries that likely won't get checked off. Don't set yourself up for failure by reaching *only* for the stars. There is a ton of low-hanging fruit for you to grab onto that has the potential to get you to your ultimate goal.

STICK WITH THIS COMPANY EVEN IF THEY REJECT YOU

Nobody wants to hear NO. The job you want may not be available right now—or there may be 70 applicants vying for it. But you still want to, and should, apply for this job.

If there is any possibility that you'll get a YES, throw your hat into the ring.

I've always used rejection as my motivation to get the next one. And just because this company is turning you down for this chance, don't give up on this company. You never know what's around the corner with this same organization that may be perfect for you. And by putting yourself in the talent pool for the first opportunity, you may automatically be considered for opportunity number two. Some of my biggest accounts are companies that said NO, NO, and then NO again—but I just knew that I could deliver for them, so I never gave up.

YOU MAY BE RIGHT AND THEY JUST DON'T SEE IT. MOVE ON

You know you're perfect for this job. Your friends know it. Your professors know it. Everybody knows it except the person interviewing you. And they just passed on you.

This is not your decision, and you need to be good with this and move on. This same company may be calling for you next week. Never burn a bridge in your mind with a company because you feel they didn't know a good thing when they had it. They know you're good.

TRUST THE PROCESS

Think you should have gotten that position and they gave it to someone else? The same company may still want you, but for a different—and possibly better—opportunity. Employers see tons of candidates. They know what they're looking for and you WILL find a home that makes sense for you and for them.

My daughter had an in with a company in New York City. Not one, but two of her mentors knew people there. So, she got a first interview. And then a second. And then a third. And by the fifth meeting, a month into the process, she felt she had met the entire company. And then the news that hurt the most:

> "We think you should apply for a different position in our company that just opened up because you're likely more qualified for that one."

No doubt that first position had been filled, but from a positive standpoint, it meant that there was still an opening. So, she started the process again—one, two, three more meetings with these people—and she finally got the job!

THERE'S ALWAYS ANOTHER WAY IN

Turned down by a lead—or just not getting a return call? Thanks to technology today, there are so many potential ways to reach somebody else at that same company whom you'd like to target. The company's website often has a list of officers. On LinkedIn you can discover others who work at that same company. Or you might even find and sign up for charitable events associated with the company. I've found myself purchasing a ticket to the In-N-Out Burger Charity Golf Tournament in the past just to get five minutes of face time with their key meeting planner.

It's all about being creative and having the will to truly give yourself a shot.

ACTION ITEM
Find one of your target companies on LinkedIn. Identify five people there whom you'd like to meet.

UPSET ABOUT HOW THAT INTERVIEW WENT? LOOK AT THE POSITIVES

Don't ever think that something you just did in furtherance of your career was a waste of time. There's no waste for positive people. Here's some of the good from what you just thought was a bad interview:

1. Out of a ton of applicants, *you* actually got an interview.

2. You likely impressed someone just now which means you've got a new fan pulling for you.

3. These interviewers likely reached out to your references—and that just proved to those already on your team that you're out there doing great things with your life.

4. Maybe *you* thought the interview went poorly, but these people may be about to make you an offer because to them it was a stellar meeting with the perfect candidate.

5. If you forgot to tell that interviewer something and you're now upset about it, don't worry. The only person who knows you omitted something is *you*.

BECOME A CHEERLEADER FOR YOUR FRIENDS

Take the time now to listen to your friends' ups and downs during this process. Cheer on their wins and help them forget the losses.

The fact that you're invested in another's success will give that friend the motivation to stick to this goal. And they, in turn, will help you.

Success is contagious. You're all in this together and you'll soon see this is true.

REMEMBER

This chapter reminded us that rejection, failure, loss, and just plain no are there to inspire you and not prevent you from achieving your goals.

The best of the best use failure and rejection for motivation. Remember that with each rejection, a new door is opened for success.

CONCLUSION

THANK YOU

I've now read this book hundreds of times and know just about every passage by heart. I certainly don't expect you to do the same. But as I read through specific sections in preparation for the many speeches that I'm privileged to give to college seniors each year, I'm reminded of just how important these simple paragraphs can be to your future. I so appreciate you giving me the chance to enter your life for just a brief moment.

I wrote this book for the love of helping others. While it's true that many before you have gone through this process alone, know that there are many hands out there willing to help. And once you're a beneficiary of advice, you'll be motivated to turn around and help another. I guess that Venus Williams story had a pretty deep impact on me after all.

THIS IS ABOUT YOU

Always remember that this quest is about you and nobody else. You need to be "the very best you" mentally and physically to make the best decisions, so first and foremost make sure to take care of yourself.

Your foundation is about to get a lot stronger, but the key for these pieces of advice is NOT for a one-time usage; this is a continual process that needs frequent re-evaluation.

I stand by the ideas in this book. They've helped me to achieve a strong level of success in my life and I am confident they'll assist you in the same manner.

But if there's one key tip that I can leave you with, it's all about the importance of keeping your pipeline loaded—regularly and often. That channel of opportunities—whether potential investors or customers for your startup or simply business prospects—needs to be filled to capacity every day, because the fact is that many will drop out. And when that happens, you need to be unaffected.

I load my pipeline with past customers because in my business, someone who's used my services three to six months ago has a new opportunity right now. And if I'm not in front of that customer on a regular basis, you can bet that my competition certainly will be.

The realization that *you're only as good as your last deal* and *there's no such thing as customer loyalty* are both offshoots of the "loading your pipeline" proposition. Once you have your pipeline loaded, you need to ask for what you want because great things won't just come to you. Even though you may think you have a dedicated and loyal customer on the hook to do business with you, the world is filled with new flavors and fresh ideas. Creativity and freshness rule here, and, honestly, once you lose a big deal that you thought you had wrapped up, you'll understand exactly what I mean.

You cannot forget about the strengths you possess that got you here.

Writing this, I'm reminded of an important sports analogy that was also one of my son's experiences from just a few years ago. Ryan's a fast ocean swimmer who started competing in triathlons when he was a senior in high school. By his first year at Boston College, Ryan's hard work had paid off. He'd become one of the top junior triathletes in America.

But there was a catch: 90% of triathletes come from a running background. And in a sport that orders swim, bike, and then run, a strong runner always has the advantage in that final kick.

Ryan knew that running was the strength of his competitors, but not *his* strength.

Fast forward to Cincinnati for the USA Triathlon Junior Nationals. There were 75 competitors vying for the National Crown. It was Ryan's final chance for a place on the podium at Nationals before aging out of juniors.

Ryan was out of the water quickly and then on the bike with the lead group. As he eyed the names on the backs of the jerseys he was surrounded by, he knew that these were all world-class runners who would smoke him on the run segment to come. With one long lap of the bike to go, Ryan's understanding of his strengths (or in this case, his non-strengths) took over and he went out on a solo breakaway to gain as best an edge as he could against the group. I was by the finish line that day when the announcer shared over the loudspeaker, "Ladies and gentlemen, it appears that Ryan Reede from Manhattan Beach, California has broken away from the lead pack on the bike." Ryan entered the final running segment of the race with a 35-second lead. One by one, the leaders picked Ryan off on the run, but he will always be the first to tell you that he did the right thing by recognizing his strengths and giving it a shot.

I'd like to leave you with the powerful words of Kenton Lee. A few years ago, Kenton traveled from his home in Boise, Idaho on a mission to help impoverished children in a village in Kenya. There, a chance meeting with a young boy wearing tattered shoes that barely fit led to a unique and special idea that continues to impress today. Knowing of the foot-borne illnesses that are prevalent in Third World countries, Kenton realized he had to do something to help this boy. He created *The Shoe That Grows*, a shoe designed to expand five sizes and last for years.

This small idea has since led to hundreds of thousands of shoes reaching kids impacted by poverty all over the world. I asked Kenton for some words of wisdom, and he wanted me to share this with you as you embark on your quest:

"I'm just a really normal guy. I never really thought I could do big things, but I knew I could do small things. And what I learned was there is power in small things. I want to encourage you as you start on your career, on your journey, don't worry about doing big things. Don't worry about having the perfect solution and making the perfect plan. Just do small things. Everybody can do a small thing. And I believe this with my whole heart: there is power in small things and small things really do make a big difference. Go out there and do some small things!"

Whether big or small, you've now set this plan of yours in motion. There's absolutely no stopping you from getting exactly what you want in life. Please know that I am always here to lend a hand and listen to your ideas and questions. Reach me anytime at Marc Reede on LinkedIn.

www.ingramcontent.com/pod-product-compliance
Lightning Source LLC
Chambersburg PA
CBHW050527100526
44581CB00009B/154/J